Universal Design in Education

Universal Design in Education

Teaching Nontraditional Students

Frank G. Bowe

BERGIN & GARVEY
Westport, Connecticut • London

Library of Congress Cataloging-in-Publication Data

Bowe, Frank.
    Universal design in education : teaching nontraditional students / Frank G. Bowe.
       p. cm.
    Includes bibliographical references and index.
    ISBN 0–89789–688–2 (alk. paper)
    1. Instructional systems—Design.   2. Educational technology.   3.
    Handicapped—Education.   4. Minorities—Education.   I. Title.
    LB1028.38.B69   2000
    371.9′045—dc21   00–031200

British Library Cataloguing in Publication Data is available.

Library of Congress Catalog Card Number: 00–031200
ISBN: 0–89789–688–2

First published in 2000

Bergin & Garvey, 88 Post Road West, Westport, CT 06881
An imprint of Greenwood Publishing Group, Inc.
www.greenwood.com

Printed in the United States of America

The paper used in this book complies with the
Permanent Paper Standard issued by the National
Information Standards Organization (Z39.48–1984).

10 9 8 7 6 5 4 3 2

To Ronald L. Mace (1947-1998)

The term "universal design" as used in this book was popularized by Ron Mace, an architect and director of the Center for Universal Design (CUD) at North Carolina State University (NCSU). Ron died on June 29, 1998. I had been with him just two weeks earlier, as he chaired a CUD advisory board meeting during the "Designing for the 21st Century" international conference on universal design, held at Hofstra University, Hempstead, Long Island, New York, where I am a professor.

Long before I ever saw anyone else use the term, Ron was writing about universal design. As early as 1990, he wrote, with two colleagues, a chapter called "Accessible Environments: Toward Universal Design" (Mace, R., Hardie, G., and Place, J., in W. E. Preiser, J. C. Vischer, and E. T. White, Eds., *Design Intervention: Toward a More Humane Architecture*. New York: Van Nostrand Reinhold). The roots that universal design has in accessibility are evident in this early use of the term. "Universal design," wrote Mace, Hardie, and Place, "means simply designing all products, buildings and exterior spaces to be usable by all people to the greatest extent possible. It is advanced here as a sensible and economical way to reconcile the artistic integrity of a design with human needs in the environment." As I was preparing this manuscript, Gregg Vanderheiden, director of the Trace R&D Center, University of Wisconsin at Madison, called my attention to an even earlier use of the term. Ron Mace, he said, had written about universal design in a 1985 document called Designers West, introducing the term this way: "Universal design is simply a way of designing a building or facility, at little or no extra cost, so that it is both attractive and functional for all people, disabled or not."

Contents

Acknowledgments

Ronald L. Mace, to whom this book is dedicated, was born in Jersey City, NJ, but raised in Winston-Salem, NC. At the age of nine, he contracted polio; from that point forward, he used wheelchairs for mobility. Ron quickly became frustrated by the architectural, transportation, and other barriers he encountered at every turn. Rather than allowing those barriers to discourage him, he set about removing them. Step one was to become an architect. He received his architecture degree from NCSU's School of Design in 1966. He then practiced architecture for four years, at which point he received an opportunity to become involved in developing one of the nation's first state accessibility building codes. Ron leaped at the chance. The North Carolina code became effective in 1974. It soon served as a model for other states.

It also served as a model for the rest of Ron's career. Beginning with Barrier Free Environments, his design consulting firm that did work for The Kennedy Center and for the Smithsonian Institution, both in Washington, DC, and other clients, and continuing with the Center for Accessible Housing at NCSU—later renamed the Center for Universal Design—Ron provided national leadership on accessibility. He was one of the "architects" behind the Fair Housing Amendments Act of 1988 (PL 100-430) and the Americans with Disabilities Act of 1990 (PL 101-336).

In the late 1980s and through most of the 1990s, Ron tirelessly promoted these ideas. As they became better-known and more widely accepted, Ron himself and CUD became nationally prominent. In his 28-year career, Ron received many awards, among them being named a Fellow of the American Institute of Architects, probably the one award that meant the most to him.

I also thank former Hofstra University associate provost Howard Negrin and provost Herman Berliner, who encouraged me to write this text; Gregg Vanderheiden, who gave me a page-by-page critique of the manuscript, together with numerous suggestions for improvement; Larry Trachtman, director of the Center for Universal Design, North Carolina State University, who offered me comments as well; and Hofstra professors Daniel Sciarra, an expert on cultural identity, and Ruth Gold, special education professor and gerontologist, who assisted me in applying the ideas of universal design to, respectively, members of ethnic/racial minority groups and to older persons.

They all told me that the subject matter of this book—how teachers and college professors can accommodate the varied needs of ever-more-diverse student bodies—is very timely. That feedback motivated me to complete the project quickly, despite many other obligations.

Finally, I express my appreciation to Greenwood Publishing Group. James Sabin, editor, encouraged me to submit the book for publication and gave me guidance on writing it. Lottie Schnell, copy editor, and Nicole Cournoyer, production editor, helped me through the painstaking work of copy editing and typesetting.

As is true with anything I write, I am the only person responsible for any errors of omission or commission in this book. My colleagues should not be blamed for any of them.

Introduction and Executive Summary

Teachers at all levels, from preschool to K–12 to university programs to adult and continuing education, now deal with a remarkably diverse student population. Growing numbers of students have such disabilities as attention deficits or learning disabilities. Many older students have impairments of hearing and of vision. Large numbers of students come from cultural traditions other than the Euro-American, Judeo-Christian Western "white" culture and for this reason bring different expectations to the classroom. Chapter 1 explores the characteristics of these non-traditional students.

Meeting all of the tremendous variety of needs these students present is not something most teachers can do. What is possible is to design and deliver instruction that responds to most of these needs. That is what this book is about.

Universal Design in Education is intended to be used as a handbook. It is not written to be read cover-to-cover. Rather, I suggest that readers spend some time with this executive summary and with Chapters 1–3, becoming familiar with (1) the concept of universal design, (2) how universal design can be applied to education, and (3) how the book is laid out. Chapters 4–7 may be consulted as needed throughout the academic year, as you encounter problems or have questions. Chapter 8, on Web pages, should be read quickly and consulted as needed when you design or update Web pages or refer your students to this or that Web address. The Resources section should be used as needed (e.g., if you want to caption a video); you will find in that section Web addresses for six (6) captioning companies.

Traditionally, what we have done in education is to accommodate individual needs, without changing courses. For example, we have told deaf students to arrange for sign language interpreters to translate the spoken lectures in the classroom. Similarly, we have relied upon students who are blind to secure Brailled or tape-recorded versions of printed materials used in class, including textbooks. One word to refer to this is "accessibility." Since 1977, schools, colleges, universities and other educational institutions have provided accommodations such as interpreters, note-takers, etc., free of charge to students as part of the institutions' obligations under federal law. Many such students have used assistive technology to facilitate their reading, writing, and other academic activities.

The 1990s movement of universal design challenges us to think again about who should be responsible for accessibility and more specifically assistive technology. Universal design asks us to look at courses, texts, schedules, and other aspects of education: Is it really necessary for teachers to present the great bulk of our instruction via speech? Isn't there a way, or aren't there several ways, for us to offer much of the same material visually (in print, on disk, etc.)? Of course, the obverse obtains as well: Must we assign only printed materials for student reading? Can't we find audible (spoken) versions, too, and make those available for people who need or prefer them?

In this book, we call taking those kinds of steps "universal design in education." Chapter 2 introduces the concept of universal design, and Chapter 3 illustrates how it may be applied to education. Succeeding chapters address different principles. Chapter 8 discusses Web-based materials. Chapter 9 brings it all together.

Universal design has several important advantages over assistive technologies. First, it is usually far less expensive than traditional steps and assistive technologies. Brailling or tape-recording of texts, and in-classroom sign language interpreting, are expensive. The State of California, in Fall 1999, ordered textbook publishers that sell texts to California schools to make available, as well, disk versions of the texts (Assembly Bill AB 422). Texts on disks can be listened to by students who are blind and by many who have learning disabilities. They may also be listened to by any student while driving. This latter advantage—an unexpected one, to be sure, but one that students quickly discover when exams loom—illustrates the beauty of universal design. Most teachers usually compose lectures on disk any-way—and with schools giving professors disks for free, it is both economical and easy for us to make one more disk copy and give that to a deaf student, lessening the note-taking burden. In both cases, accommodating for different needs by planning in advance makes instruction available for more students, at lower costs, and reduces the need for after-the-fact steps such as interpreting and Brailling or tape-recording of printed materials.

As these examples illustrate, universal design is a design approach that maximizes usability of products, services, and environments for every-one—young people and old, short people and tall, people with disabilities and without. The idea is that with universal design, only a small minority of students will need "special" accommodations—those who cannot use even universally designed instruction.

The concept of universal design first arose in design of the built environment, where it was employed to market homes (in particular) as responding to "life-span" needs. That is, a universally designed home is one that young children and senior citizens alike find comfortable and convenient, yet adolescents and working-age adults also find appealing. As people aged, they would feel no need to move, because the house posed no barriers to them. Thus, universal design was initially conceived as a marketing theme: it took the idea of "accessibility" (which carries connotations of disability and of government-mandated design features) and presented it as something that appeals to all of us, that is, as an approach that we would elect to use because it responds to our enlightened understanding of diverse needs.

The concept then was adopted by makers of personal-use products, including kitchen utensils, room temperature controls, desk lamps, and the like. In the minds of Ron Mace, founder of the Center for Universal Design (CUD) at North Carolina State University, and his colleagues, the idea was that if usability could be marketed to the general public as convenient, it would sell itself. People who try wide-grip scissors or other kitchen utensils, such as Friendly Fit^{tm} forks and spoons, that are sold in Home Depot and Williams-Sonoma household supply stores, often prefer them to conventional implements: they just feel better. That was Ron's idea: if he could present universal design so that people would voluntarily adopt it, the world would become a much more livable place for all of us.

Under Ron's leadership, CUD developed seven principles of universal design. Here is a brief summary:

1. The design can be used by, and marketed to, all kinds of people. A good example is power doors which open automatically when someone steps on a pressure-sensitive area on the pathway leading to the door.
2. The design incorporates a wide variety of preferences. People have choices in how they use it. An example is an ATM machine that lets people decide whether to read or listen to information.
3. The product or service is easy to understand and use. It avoids unnecessary complexity. A good example is the user manuals that accompany Hewlett-Packard printers—they are very brief and clear.
4. It works in all kinds of settings. Even in eyes-busy or noisy environments, people can use it with ease. An example is an information system at a train station that offers arrival/departure information in both visual and auditory modes.
5. The design accommodates error. People can make a mistake without disastrous consequences. An example is a kiosk that offers the option at every screen of returning to the main menu.
6. The product or service requires minimal effort to use. Neither intense nor sustained physical effort is   needed. Door levers are an excellent example—no grasping or twisting motions are required.

7. It accommodates variations in size and position. People can use it while standing, sitting, or reaching. An example is subway turnstiles that present the token or card slot at a height easily reached by people using wheelchairs and young children, yet do not require ambulatory adults to crouch.

What does universal design tell us to do as teachers? The principles of universal design place responsibility for making curricula, materials, and environments accessible to and usable by all students upon the teacher and the school. As educators, we need to consider ways to make education more convenient for time-pressed students, more comfortable for people from diverse backgrounds, and more flexible for persons having different learning styles.

A teacher preparing universally designed curricula and materials will:

• Present information in multiple ways. Anything written or otherwise offered visually is also spoken aloud, and vice versa. The teacher, recognizing that personal computers and software provide easy and rapid ways to customize how information is presented, not only prepares curricula, materials, hand outs, etc., on disk but also makes those disks available to students on request (so they can make large-print versions, etc.) and posts them on Web pages where they may be read by students using their personal adaptive equipment. Teachers may also take advantage of such tools as the eReader, from the Center for Applied Special Technology, *www.cast.org*; this software adds voice, highlights text, and reduces support for students as they become more independent.

• Offer multiple ways for students to interact with and respond to curricula and materials. Students may respond by speaking (e.g., in class, into a tape recorder, to a computer program, etc.), writing, typing, etc. Students may also control the "look" of information (type size, font, foreground and background colors, etc.) and the pace at which material is presented on a computer.

• Provide multiple ways for students to find meaning in the material and thus motivate themselves. Students may work independently, may work as members of a team, and may show that they have mastered principles by applying those to favorite activities (e.g., calculate batting averages to demonstrate knowledge of adding, dividing, etc.). Some students may benefit from participating in an instructor-sponsored listserv, through which students may post comments, questions, etc., to each other and to the instructor, while others may learn well through group study listservs that allow student-only interaction via e-mail.

- Make good use of personal and course Web pages. Web pages can easily be made interactive, greatly adding to students' benefit. Information on a Web page may be read using the students' own, personal adaptive technology devices and equipment at home. Teachers must ensure that such Web pages comply with the World Wide Web Consortium (W3C) access guidelines (*www.w3.org/wai*). One convenient way to check such compliance is to use "Bobby" (see *www.cast.org/bobby*). Bobby is a computer software program that evaluates the accessibility of Web pages and offers specific suggestions for improvement.

What else will educators teaching in universally designed ways do?

TIP SHEET: UNIVERSALLY DESIGNED TEACHING

1. Become aware of your own culture's teachings and how those affect you as an educator. Then learn how the cultures of your students may predispose them to approach education differently. In particular, examine the place of time, the relative importance of academic work v. family needs if/when the two conflict, and individual v. group achievements. As a product of Eurocentric cultures, I automatically value promptness in my students, expect them to complete their academic work even if family needs intervene, and measure performance by each student individually. Those are my biases. When I have students who come from other cultural traditions, I need to recognize that their values may well differ from mine; occasionally, I bend and sometimes I expect them to. (Details: Chapter 1.)

2. Provide students with options for demonstrating knowledge and skills. Those options should include not only traditional tests and term papers but also group activities, demonstration via activities in the community and/or in the classroom, and portfolios of achievements. This rich variety of alternatives responds to variances in student learning styles and preferences. (Details: Chapter 1.)

3. Offer instruction, and accept student work, at a distance. Attending class in person is not an option for some people; it is inconvenient for others. Today, e-mail, the Web, and the increasing availability of broadband telecommunications (which transports voice, video, and data over the same phone line at the same time) make distance learning a viable alternative for many people. (Details: Chapter 3.)

4. Alert students to availability of digitized texts (e-books). Not all distance-learning students will need them, but some will, and so will some students who are blind or have dyslexia: the already enormous volume of electronic (digital) books and other reading materials offers exciting options for universally designing instruction. (Details: Chapter 3.)

5. Offer students information in redundant media. Your lectures were prepared on disk; make a disk copy available. Upload the lecture and other handouts to your Web page, where students can read them using personal adaptive technologies such as screen enlargers and speech synthesis. Very important: the same information should be offered in both ways. This includes things you say or show in class. (Details: Chapters 4 and 5.)

6. Provide the support students need to improve accuracy and speed. For example, some students do far better when they can dictate something than when they write or type it. Computer speech recognition has matured to the point that it understands one person's voice quite well and thus may be used for dictation. (Details: Chapter 4.)

7. Translate important materials to other languages as needed by your students. Computer software that translates between English and other language has matured to the point that it provides "draft quality" translations. Ask a colleague who is fluent in the target language to polish the product. (Details: Chapter 5.)

8. Choose physically accessible locations for your classes. If you have a choice, elect rooms with desks/chairs that are movable rather than one with fixed seats. (Details: Chapter 7.)

Chapter 1

Diverse Students

Writing in late 1999 for Long Island's newspaper *Newsday*, Saul Friedman recounted the story of two senior citizens who signed up for a course at a community college. At the first class meeting, Friedman wrote, the teacher intoned: "This is not a course for seniors. Seniors think more slowly and can't absorb at the speed of the other students. I won't slow down for you people." That attitude is diametrically opposed to the spirit which infuses this book. As educators, we not only should accommodate nontraditional students; we will find, often to our own surprise, that by doing so, we enrich the educational experience for all our students.

Ironically, Friedman went on to observe that the community college teacher had been "overwhelmed" by the "unexpected number" of seniors who enrolled in the course. He should not have been surprised. At the turn of the century, much of the growth in education is directly due to increased numbers of nontraditional students. To meet their needs, we need to apply the teachings of "universal design" to education. The Baby Boom generation, a 76-million strong cohort often described as a "pig in a python" because it is so much bigger than the generations before and after it, has already reached their 50s. Over the next 30 years, Boomers will retire and the number of elderly Americans will double. Already, the demographics of higher education have changed considerably. A generation ago, virtually all university students were in the 18 to 24-year-old cohort; today, those young adults represent just over half of the undergraduate population. According to *The Chronicle of Higher Education Almanac* (August 26, 1998), in 1995 (the latest year for which data were available), 57% of students in higher education were 18–24 years of age, 40% were 25–49, and 4% were over 50 years of age. The latter two proportions will increase, while the former one will decrease, over the foreseeable future. Among other factors driving this trend is the growing importance of information in American society. Increasingly rare is the person who stays in one profession for his or her entire career; much more common now is career-shifting. Even for people who continue in one occupation for several decades, life-long learning is imperative. To a degree my father would have found unimaginable, knowledge in virtually every field of study has exploded. The only way we can adapt to that frantic pace is to continue educating ourselves.

In a now-famous effort to understand how America treats older people, Patricia Moore, then 25, disguised herself as a woman of 85: she not only donned grey wigs, wore makeup to wrinkle her face and hands, and dressed in out-of-fashion garments, as one might imagine, but she also used devices that worsened her hearing and blurred her vision, while also using prosthetics to stiffen her arm and leg joints. Over a period of three years, she traveled to 116 cities in North America, spending untold hours talking with older people and living side-by-side with them. Among the results of this project are Moore inventions that are widely recognized today as exemplars of universal design: the "Good Grip" kitchen utensils (with big foam handles) and a pill bottle that resets its timer each time it is opened. She is now a design consultant in Phoenix, Arizona.

What are the lessons Moore and others have taught us? When we talk about universal design in education meeting diverse needs, what are the needs we are discussing and how many people have such needs? These are questions about demographics (the study of populations) and of prevalence (how many individuals have a particular condition or need). There is another term, "incidence," which refers to how many additional people develop a certain condition in any given year; that is helpful information but not of primary concern to us here.

Overall, we are talking about some 54 million Americans who have limitations of activity, of whom about 26 million have severe or profound limitations. (Unless otherwise noted, all numbers in this book refer to the United States of America.) The most common limitations in children and youth are specific learning disabilities, mental retardation, emotional disturbance, and attention deficits. The most frequent among college-age and other young adults are specific learning disabilities, attention deficits, and various levels of emotional disturbance or mental illness. Among adults in the middle-age years (25–54), the most-seen limitations are physical (mobility) conditions and health impairments. The most common limitations among persons over age 65 are physical (mobility) conditions, health impairments, and sensory limitations (including blindness and other loss of vision and deafness and other loss of hearing). The fastest-growing age group in America is that of people older than 85; of them, half need assistance with eating, dressing, shopping and other everyday tasks. When people, of whatever age, have severe or profound limitations of activity, regardless of type, we say they have "disabilities."

We are also talking about individuals from ethnic/racial minority cultures. This includes some 31 million Americans who are persons of Hispanic origin; they comprise about 11% of the population and represent the single fastest-growing ethnic minority group in the United States. According to the U.S. Bureau of the Census (which is the major source of the demographic data in this chapter), persons of Hispanic origin probably will become larger in number than African Americans some time early in this new century. In addition, we also are talking about African Americans (35 million, or 13% of the American population), Asian Americans and Pacific Islanders (11 million, or 4% of the population) and Native Americans (American Indians; 2.4 million, or 1% of the total). All numbers are estimates made by the Census Bureau in July 1999 (*www.census.gov/population/estimates/nation/*). A recent report from the U.S. Department of Labor (*Futurework: Trends and Challenges for Work in the 21st Century*, 1999) echoes these facts: over the next 50 years, minority groups taken as a whole will gradually increase in size until they comprise half of the U.S. population. Persons of Hispanic origin (who may be of any race) will constitute some 25% of all Americans by the year 2050. Many will be immigrants: the U.S. population is projected to grow 50% in those years, with two-thirds of the increase due to immigration.

Are members of ethnic and racial minority groups "nontraditional" in education? On the whole, yes, especially in higher education. The *Futurework* report from the U.S. Department of Labor reveals that just 62% of adolescents of Hispanic origin complete high school each year. While African Americans graduate from high school about as often as do whites, they are less likely to complete four years of college. These facts are troubling in today's "information economy," which places a premium upon high levels of education and training.

We are talking, as well, about people who have different learning styles. Some people learn best by listening to information, others by reading it, and yet others by participating in activities. Notably, some members of ethnic/racial minority groups tend to learn better in collaborative endeavors than in individualized ones. Finally, we are talking about people who find traditional education inconvenient for one reason or another: parents of young children, people who live far away from educational institutions, people who travel a great deal, etc. There are no reliable estimates of the numbers of such individuals.

The different statistics cannot simply be added, of course. Many older Americans also have limitations; some persons of Hispanic origin are also people with disabilities and some are over 65 years of age. Taking these overlaps into consideration, and remembering that we are not able at this time to quantify the number of people who have learning styles or preferences that do not mesh with traditional teaching techniques, we can estimate that about 60 million Americans of all ages, or some 22% of the nation's population, is in one way or another "diverse" as that term is used in this book. The point is a basic one: educators at all levels, from preschool through college to adult and continuing education, can expect to encounter sizeable numbers of individuals who have needs or preferences (or both) that make the traditional oral-lecture plus assigned-reading format of instruction problematic or difficult for them. Universal design in education tells educators to prepare, in advance, for these very different needs and, to the extent feasible, design and deliver instruction so as to meet those needs.

PEOPLE WITH DISABILITIES

The group of individuals with the most evident and pressing needs for universal design in education are persons who have disabilities. In demographics, we use "disability" to refer to permanent medical conditions that significantly limit people's abilities to engage in everyday activities. This definition helps us to estimate demand for accommodations in education, because going to school, reading, writing, and the like, are important activities of daily life. However, aside from demographics, we should think differently about people with disabilities. Gregg Vanderheiden, director of the Trace R&D Center at the University of Wisconsin at Madison, is fond of saying that "disability is something you experience, not something you are." What he means is that someone like me (I am deaf) will experience problems in one situation (I won't hear auditory alarms, for example) but not in others (deafness does not affect me in any way as I type this on my PC). Stated differently, as I did some 22 years ago (Bowe, 1978): disability is an interaction between a person and an environment. It is not, in this understanding, a medical condition. Why does this matter? It matters because it tells us that if we modify the educational environment, even in small ways, students with disabilities will not encounter problems, or will face far fewer problems. We call the process of doing that "universal design in education."

The U.S. Bureau of the Census has estimated that 54 million Americans of all ages have disabilities; that is 20% or one in every five Americans, given a national population, as of July 1999, of 273 million. The Census Bureau defines disability as a limitation in a functional activity (e.g., seeing, walking) or in a socially defined role or task (e.g., working, going to school); in addition, people who received government assistance because of disability were included. Nearly 26 million individuals had severe disabilities or limitations that made them unable to perform everyday activities. They represent about 9.9% of all Americans, or about one in every ten (McNeil, 1997, Table 1, p. 6). As large as it is, the number of Americans with disabilities rises year after year. The U.S. population of individuals with disabilities is growing by about one-half million persons every year.

An earlier study helps to cast some light on the needs of people with disabilities. Looking at people aged 15 and over who reported any kind of functional limitation, the U.S. Census Bureau reported in 1993 that:

- 17 million had difficulty walking as much as a city block and 9 million could not do that at all;
- of the 16 million who had difficulty lifting and carrying a weight of ten pounds or more, 8 million could not do this at all;
- of the 11 million who had difficulty understanding conversations, 900,000 could not hear them at all; and
- 10 million had difficulty reading the words and letters in ordinary newsprint and 1.6 million could not read them at all. (McNeil, 1993, Table B, p. 6)

In general, the number of such individuals increases as ages rise; other than mental retardation and other learning-related conditions, disabilities usually are acquired rather than congenital (present at birth). Fewer than 3% of young children under three years of age have a disability. About 11% of those in K–12 programs do. The rate of disability leaps once people pass 50 years of age. Among persons aged 55 to 64, 36.6%, or more than one out of every three, have a disability, as do almost half (47%) of individuals aged 65 to 79 (McNeil, 1997, Table 1, p. 6).

The kinds of disabilities people have differ by age range. About one-tenth of all K-12 students have disabilities. The most common are "specific learning disabilities"—conditions which make reading, doing math, and organizing difficult. Learning disabilities are also common in the college-age population. Substantial numbers of children, youth, and adults have attention deficit disorder (ADD), with or without hyperactivity. Adult/continuing education programs, by contrast, will often see participants with hearing and vision limitations; these conditions are much less prevalent in children, youth, and young adults. They will also find substantial numbers of students having physical disabilities that make getting around at least somewhat problematic. While the absolute number of older students who have learning disabilities or attention deficits is large, their prominence in adult/continuing education programs is reduced by the much-larger presence of older people having physical or sensory limitations. Gregg Vanderheiden, writing in the early 1990s during the heyday of the television series "Thirty Something," penned a summary he called "Thirty Something (Million): Should They Be Exceptions?" (*www.trace.wisc.edu/docs/30-some*). This paper has good charts illustrating these differences by age range.

Teachers in K-12 schools will be informed of any disabilities the children may have, usually by the principal, who receives this information from the Individualized Education Program (IEP) Team that develops the child's individual plan for learning, called the IEP. In college and thereafter, however, it is the student's responsibility to alert the educator to any special needs. (I ask, in the first class of each semester: "If any of you has a special need, please e-mail me or see me after class." This lets them know I expect them to tell me, yet it avoids embarrassment.)

Learning Disabilities

Specific learning disabilities are conditions in which information is somehow "messed up" in the brain. People with specific learning disabilities hear what teachers say, and see what authors write, but by the time the data are perceived, or interpreted, in the brain, something happens. In dyslexia, printed letters and symbols may seem to turn upside down or even to float across the page. In other kinds of learning disabilities, words the teacher says are not understood with certainty. The student may ask himself, "Was that 'draw' I just heard? Or was it 'raw'? Or 'flaw'?" In yet other instances, students may not be able to separate "signal" from "field" (or, to use different terms, "figure" from "ground"); these individuals have difficulty isolating the information that is of educational interest from surrounding but largely irrelevant information.

There are a number of things educators can do. Unfortunately for teachers, students with learning disabilities vary tremendously one from another. For one student, providing information on disk suffices; this student listens to material rather than (or in addition to) reading it. He or she uses speech synthesis software and hardware that is installed on a personal PC. The same technologies help students who are blind or have low vision. The synthesizer's hardware provides the voice; the software tells that voice what to read, how to read it, how fast to read it, etc. A phenomenal amount of digitized material that can be read using speech synthesizers is now available. One source is *www.rfbd.org* (Recording for the Blind and Dyslexic), which offers digitized versions of thousands of publications and materials. Increasingly, mainstream publishers also offer disk-based versions of textbooks. (The Resources section that follows Chapter 9 contains a list of many online sources of digitized texts.)

For other students, however, advance organizers are needed; these students benefit from having scaffolding that helps them to make sense out of large amounts of information. Yet other students with learning disabilities need extra time to complete assignments or to take tests. I suggest you ask the student: "What can I do?" In addition to taking the steps the student requests (extra time on tests, etc.), teachers should repeat key points and give examples. All of this helps students who have difficulty processing rapidly presented auditory information. The pace of instruction should also be slowed down, but in a specific way: try for rapidly spoken but short sentences, and pause between them. Do not slow down within a sentence, or within a concept or idea; that actually diminishes comprehension by many students having learning disabilities or mental retardation. (I also avoid displaying certain words on an overhead, or with Powerpoint[tm], while speaking different words. This can cause consternation among some students with learning disabilities, who must decide whether to read the displayed words or to listen to my spoken words. See Chapter 5.)

Attention Deficit Disorder and Attention Deficit Hyperactivity Disorder

ADD and ADHD differ from learning disabilities in that attention-related conditions render the student temporarily "unavailable for learning." In ADD, the student may appear to be day-dreaming for short periods of time; in ADHD, the student is so busy doing other things that he does not attend adequately to the learning task. (In learning disabilities, to articulate the distinction, the student is available for learning; in ADD and ADHD, much important information is simply not received, so it is not learned.)

What a teacher can do with ADD/ADHD students is to slow down (again, between but not within key ideas), repeat, and give examples. By slowing down after presenting major concepts, the educator gives students extra opportunities to attend to the necessary information. Behavior modification techniques, such as reinforcement for appropriate behavior, are also helpful. With adults, this is more subtle than it often is with children. (Sometimes I give my lecture standing near a student who appears to be daydreaming; by being near her, I assure that the eyes of other students are turned in the direction of the wayward student. I need do nothing more.)

Hearing Loss

Impairments of hearing are quite common in adult/continuing education programs. We use the term "deaf" if someone cannot understand the spoken word through the ear alone, no matter how much amplification is used; the term "hard of hearing" applies if people can understand some things through the ear alone, with amplification. Hearing loss is much less frequent in K–12 or college classes. The way we traditionally have delivered education—a teacher lectures to a class of note takers—places these people at a disadvantage. It only takes one missed word, or a few, to alter the entire meaning of a sentence. (Consider, for example: "Character was central to Henry James's narrative technique" v. "Character wasn't central to Henry James's narrative technique.") For students with more severe hearing losses, particularly those that occurred early in life, a second, educationally significant, limitation is one of not having mastered the English language. When one is deaf or severely hard-of-hearing from early in life, learning language is extremely difficult.

Teachers having hard-of-hearing or deaf students in their classes should make material that is delivered auditorially also available visually. An educator can give the student a disk or a printout containing that day's lecture as prepared for delivery; this greatly reduces the amount of note-taking needed, a big help because one cannot simultaneously look down to write notes and look up to lipread or watch an interpreter. Teachers should also take care to face the class when speaking; avoid speaking to the blackboard. Also stay away from bright windows or other light sources (when strong light is behind you, it casts your face into shadows, making it almost impossible for anyone to lipread you). If you show a video, use a captioned one. (The Resources section, after Chapter 9, has information on six captioning organizations.)

Blindness and Low Vision

Visual impairment, like hearing loss, is most frequent among older persons. We use the term "blindness" when people have vision that measures 20/200 or worse, or when their range of vision is sharply restricted; "low vision" refers to measured vision that is 20/70 at best to 20/200 at worst, or the range is limited but not as much as in the case of blindness. The major difficulty students who are blind or have low vision encounter in education is in reading assigned materials. They may also have problems taking notes, but most individuals who have lived with a vision impairment for some time have figured out effective ways of doing that.

Physical Disabilities

Physical disabilities are relatively uncommon in people under the age of about 50. When they do occur, the major effects tend to be ones that interfere with mobility, or make it very difficult. These students may have problems getting to class, especially during winter months. They may require a little extra time to move from class to class. Some, particularly people who have cerebral palsy, encounter problems in taking notes. At any given moment in time, very large numbers of Americans have temporary limitations—they may break a leg, for example. We define "temporary" as lasting six or fewer months. If you have students who sustain injuries during a course term, you may need to make short-term adaptations. These may include relocating the class, at least temporarily, to a ground-floor room or even to another, more accessible, building. You can also give students a little advice: Wheelchairs can be rented for as little as $5 a day. Scooters (battery-powered carts) are somewhat more expensive. Crutches are even less expensive; forearm crutches are a good choice, because they are easier to use than are full-length crutches and because they do not (as regular crutches do) cause underarm discomfort. Walkers are excellent mobility aids; although most people associate them with elderly residents of nursing homes, the fact is that walkers provide very good stability, easy maneuverability, and ready storage when not in use. Among others, Maddak (1-800-443-4926, *www.maddak.com*), North Coast Medical (1-800-821-9319, *www.ncmedical.com*), and Sammons Preston (1-800-323-5547, *www.sammonspreston.com*) have daily living aids, including some that assist in academic work (reading, writing, etc.). In addition, follow the suggestions in Chapter 7 (Principle Seven).

Teachers having students with disabilities, whether permanent or temporary, should first of all ensure that the classroom building, and the room itself, are physically accessible. This means doors that are at least 36 inches wide, building entrances that are flush with outdoor walkways, elevators in multi-story buildings, and the like (see Chapter 7). Educators should also consider distance learning techniques, especially two-way video, to relieve the student's mobility problems, particularly in inclement weather (see Chapter 6).

MEMBERS OF ETHNIC/RACIAL MINORITY CULTURES

According to Nathan Shedroff (1997), writing in a recent report from the National Academy of Sciences (Biermann, 1997), a critical issue in design of information systems is

> how they address people from different backgrounds and culture since the next level of computer users (the next 100 million users) will not be as willing to change their approach to problems and their interaction with devices as the enthusiasts and professionals who comprise the present base of computer users. Issues of language, gesture, understanding, privacy, approach, civility, and "life" are not consistent throughout the world—and wonderfully so—and must be discovered and documented. (p. 10)

He might have been writing about education in general, not just about information technologies. What are the issues Shedroff and others have identified that relate to education of people who come from minority cultures? To answer this question, we need to recognize, first, something that Hofstra professor Daniel Sciarra (1999) has emphasized: Americans from minority cultural backgrounds vary greatly in the extent to which they identify with "old country" values v. the degree to which they have assimilated aspects of the dominant American culture. That is, they differ in the extent to which they are acculturated to dominant American cultures. We cannot simply say, Dr. Sciarra tells us, that someone is from a particular culture and therefore espouses certain beliefs. Rather, we must strive to understand how that particular person thinks and behaves, realizing that he or she may move, over time, along a continuum from the "old culture" to the "new" one. That is, Americans who are members of ethnic groups vary within themselves, over time, in the degree to which their interests, preferences, and beliefs are shaped by one culture or another. Accordingly, of course, they also vary between themselves.

One important factor to watch is the pluralistic or collectivist orientation of many minority cultures, which contrasts sharply with the focus on the individual of the Euro-American culture. Almost without thinking about it, those of us belonging to the dominant culture call attention to individual achievement. We stress it in the ways we teach. We test for it. We celebrate it when we find it. One small example: we start classes at a certain time, whether or not everyone has arrived. Another, also small, example: we expect a student to complete his or her work on a timely basis, even if personal or family emergencies make that difficult. Those expectations, together with others (see discussion of nonverbal communication, below), are viewed by many members of ethnic and racial minority groups as comprising a "negative attitude" by "the educational elite" (Parette, 1999; Salend and Taylor, 1993).

For many cultures, all of this emphasis upon individual accomplishment may actually be offensive. They place a lot less stress upon the individual and much more upon the group, especially the family. They consider it appropriate to begin a meeting, not at some artificial time, but when all of the important participants have arrived. They believe that the health and well-being of people and their families override artificial deadlines, such that if there is a family emergency, the student should attend to that, and be praised for doing so, notwithstanding the fact that the academic work must be postponed. Similarly, members of some of these minority groups learn much better when they are given opportunities to be team members than when they are required to work, and are tested, separately.

There are also different modes of nonverbal communication. One example is how personal space is interpreted. Some minority cultures teach that it is entirely appropriate for people to spend their days in very close physical proximity—so close, in fact, that some members of the dominant American culture become distinctly uncomfortable. In other cultures (Muslim Indian culture springs to mind), physical proximity and interpersonal contact may be frowned upon. Some cultures teach that it is a mark of respect for students to avoid direct eye gaze at their teachers—while majority educators expect, and even demand, that students make eye contact with them. Body language means different things in different cultures. If I were to stand ramrod-straight when meeting someone from Japan, for example, I would be showing disrespect; the exact same body posture when meeting a majority-culture individual could signal the opposite—respect. (I think of how I am when I'm in a room with Hofstra's president. I tend to hold back a little and allow him the prerogative of noticing and recognizing me; I would not feel comfortable, as a university professor, making the first move by stepping closer to him or initiating the conversation with him.) To take another example: expressive communication for many African Americans is not exclusively verbal; rather, bodily movements convey considerable meaning. Many whites, by contrast, will "let the words speak for themselves."

The availability of instructional materials in different languages is an important concern. It is not simply that books, articles, handouts, etc., may need to be translated from English; it is also that the nuances of languages be respected. Simple word-for-word translations may result in serious mis-communication. A good example is that given above: if written materials talk about individual empowerment and individual achievement, but do not explain that we intend no disrespect for group empowerment and group achievement, some students may be confused or even disturbed. Shedroff (1997) added, in his paper for the National Academy of Science's *Screen Deep* report, that "automatic language translation is one of the most critical—and difficult

—problems to solve" (p. 10). This is so for several reasons. First, minority group members may not learn about educational opportunities on a timely basis, because publicity about the programs is offered only in English. That includes the topics, content, intended audiences, dates, times, etc., of courses, whether the information is promoted in print or on the Web. This is a very major problem for anyone who is concerned, as I am, about making the benefits of education more widely available. Second, more obviously, texts and other reading materials often are available only in English. When I test Spanish–primary students using tests in English, I have to be skeptical about the results. Finally, communication in the classroom, both professor-to-student and student-to-classmates and -professor, generally is in English. Automatic language translation (see Chapter 5) promises to help us to solve many of these problems.

Some cultures teach that the family, and not society at large, is responsible for family members who have disabilities or other limitations of activity. Some African-American families regard government as being quite appropriately responsible for meeting the special needs of people with disabilities, especially children and older individuals; some Hispanic families, by contrast, believe that it is the family that must meet those needs. These families may feel embarrassment about children with disabilities. (In 20-plus years as a consultant to the U.S. Census Bureau, I have continually found that Hispanic families under-report disability. They do not acknowledge it to census takers [who are seen as representatives of government]. This produces consistently low estimates about how many people of Hispanic origin have disabilities. I have to mentally adjust the reported numbers, recognizing that some degree of under-reporting likely has occurred.) Some cultures (one that comes to mind is that of first-generation Italian families) hold superstitions in far higher regard than does the dominant American culture. Members of these families may fear that if someone voluntarily participates in an experiential activity intended to help that person to appreciate what it is to have a disability, this person is "tempting fate." (I have had students complain to me about such experiential activities, citing their parents' objections.)

A related concern of some families is that technology may call unwanted attention to family members. This is particularly the case with respect to assistive technology used by persons with disabilities. However, the worry is a broader one. Consider, as one example, interactive video technologies, such as those used in distance learning (see Chapter 6). Educators need to be sensitive to the fact that, for some families, the very idea that a video camera would capture the family's living quarters, and show those to other people, is unacceptable. In some instances, that is because it seems to be an unwarranted invasion of privacy; in others, it could be a source of shame. There is more to it than this. While members of the dominant Euro-American culture may feel perfectly comfortable with cell phones, beepers, etc., in public places such as classrooms and restaurants, for members of some minority culture groups just the ringing of a cell phone or the beeping of a pager, let alone holding a conversation over a cell phone in a public place, would be a cause for embarrassment. The need to preserve the family's self-esteem is high in many such cultures, so a premium is placed upon avoiding unnecessary public attention. Of course, when a family member requires assistive technology because of disability, the fact that the device calls public attention to the disability could be viewed by some family members as even more humiliating.

What are some steps that educators can take to respond to these concerns? It is my belief that the first such step must be to reflect upon our own cultural heritages and upon our beliefs about people from other cultures. Such self-awareness is a critical component of cultural competence. I have to consciously remind myself that my typical obsession with time (I am early to class, I start class at the assigned time, etc.) is a reflection of my cultural upbringing; I have to bear in mind that there is nothing "natural" or "right" about these attitudes of mine and that there are, rather, other views that are equally valid about the place of time in our everyday lives.

Similarly, for me, as a person who has had a disability for a half century, disabilities are not conditions that I regard with shame. The fact that I had measles when I was very young, and was given a "miracle drug" that only later became recognized as having a side-effect of causing deafness, is not something that embarrasses me. I didn't choose to take mycin drugs, so why should I want to hide my deafness? (My colleague Dr. Sciarra, an expert on acculturation, tells me that my attitudes reflect my personal level of adjustment to deafness. He draws parallels between that and the varying degrees to which members of immigrant families acculturate to the dominant American culture. I suspect he's right.) Nonetheless, in my efforts to be culturally sensitive and competent, I have to acknowledge that some other cultures do in fact teach that deafness (and other disabilities) are causes of shame. This knowledge helps me to deal with families that shrink from public acknowledgment of disability—it teaches me to approach such families with care, giving them time to get to know and trust me, before I ask them to consider public services for their child. Beth Harry, Maya Kalyanpur, and Monimahka Day (1999) have called this "cultural reciprocity," their term for how educators and family members learn to understand each other and to appreciate what each has to offer to children. To pick up on the distance-learning problem discussed earlier, I would show some sensitivity if I were to make available to students the option of using voice telephone connections rather than video telephony to "attend" my lectures; voice phone connections are much less invasive of a family's privacy than are video connections.

A third step is to assess all key components of the educational program for possible cultural insensitivity. Hofstra professor Eduardo Duarte has been particularly vocal about the cultural insensitivity of American public schools (Duarte and Smith, 2000). To take an example discussed briefly above: do meetings always start at the scheduled time, or is flexibility allowed in respect for cultural differences about time? There are, of course, occasions when promptness is necessary, but, as Duarte and Smith teach us, there are also times when it is not. Students and members of their families might be asked to review the program to suggest improvements. Take, as another example, avoidance of eye gaze, an issue raised earlier. I use eye contact as a way to reassure myself throughout a lecture that my students are understanding the ideas I am trying to teach them; I quickly see, in their eyes, confusion, boredom, etc., and that alters the manner, and the pace, in which I teach. I have to remind myself, when I have minority-culture students, that they may keep their eyes down as a sign of respect. If so, I will sometimes say to them: "Thank you for this gesture of respect. I appreciate it. However, this is my classroom, and I ask that you maintain eye contact with me during class. I need that, to monitor my own teaching. I assure you that you will not be showing me any disrespect by doing this."

It should be obvious, but it bears mentioning anyway: educational programs should recruit a culturally diverse staff. The "feeling" that students and potential students get about programs often has its roots in the kinds of people they see when they visit the program (Duarte and Smith, 2000; Harry, Kalyanpur, and Day, 1999). Similarly, a culturally diverse staff is more capable than is a culturally monotonous staff of keeping everyone aware of cultural sensitivities and of training others in cultural competence (Sciarra, 1999). To illustrate: one step that culturally diverse personnel might suggest to resolve a family's embarrassment about assistive technology is to arrange for the family to see other families from the same culture using such technologies (Parette, 1999).

DIFFERENT LEARNING STYLES

I am the only deaf professor at Hofstra, a university having 500 full-time professors and another 600 adjunct (part-time) instructors. Unlike most of my colleagues on campus, I learn best by reading, alone. They tend to learn best by listening and by interacting with other people. They enjoy going to conferences and conventions. I don't; I attend such gatherings only if I am a scheduled speaker. This is a learning-style difference, despite the fact that in this case it is traceable to the facts that I can't hear and that I grew up learning this way, because there were no interpreters in my elementary, secondary, or college classes. There are, nonetheless, people whose hearing is not impaired who learn well with this same learning style. Traditional education, featuring as it does a teacher lecturing aurally to a room filled with listeners, is not readily amenable to that kind of learning.

There are, of course, people who learn very differently from the way I do. For them, the traditional textbook, supplemented by instructor hand-outs in class, assigned journal articles, et cetera, features too much reading. Some would rather participate in experiences, learning by doing. Some would enjoy listening to texts, articles, and other information sources. In fact, I have friends who are blind who tell me that their ideal learning mode is to play back an audio tape at twice to three times normal conversational speed. They use tape recorders having very rapid playback speeds (350 words per minute to 500 or even more words per minute). By listening to information at those speeds, these blind students force themselves to really concentrate. They report to me that their memories are far sharper, simply because of that intense concentration.

PEOPLE FOR WHOM TRADITIONAL APPROACHES ARE INCONVENIENT

An unknown number—but a growing one—of Americans find traditional times, locations, and even formats of education to be inconvenient. As a professor teaching graduate students at Hofstra, I am accustomed to meeting in person with my students once each week, for slightly under two hours each time. My colleagues who have classes with undergraduates see them twice weekly, for even shorter periods of time. This calendar is more than a century old. (That's why it is so impervious to change!) Yet for many people, it's a very inconvenient plan. Far better, for some, would be three-hour classes, every other week, so that fewer commutes to and from campus would be required. Some of those same people would find distance learning (see Chapter 6) even more convenient, because it would require very little, or actually no, commuting. Distance learning uses telecommunications technologies to deliver instruction at a distance. This holds obvious appeal for parents with very young children, older adults who risk injury when they travel during inclement weather, and people with severe disabilities or health conditions who cannot commute at all or only with great difficulty and at great expense.

Distance learning also appeals to individuals for whom traditional education is inconvenient because it disrupts family routines. Recalling that for some cultures, in a conflict between the quality of family life, on the one hand, and the level of academic achievement of an individual family member, on the other, the family's needs outweigh the individual's, we can begin to understand that traditional approaches to education that place stress upon other family members might be perceived as harmful. Alternatives to traditional approaches may minimize such stress. This raises, as do some of the other accommodations discussed in this book, conflicts in K–12 teachers and in college or university professors. I can understand such approach-avoidance conflicts. On the one hand, I want each of my students to be comfortable with my teaching and capable of performing at their optimal levels in my courses. On the other hand, however, I am a university professor. My role in my students' lives is to be a teacher and a guide. How to resolve such conflicts? I believe that, at minimum, those of us who teach should be aware of, and sensitive to, the dictates of different cultures, even if we insist that students from those cultures adhere to our standards while they are in our educational programs.

Chapter 2

Seven Principles of Universal Design

In 1995, the Center for Universal Design (CUD) at North Carolina State University in Raleigh, NC, brought together ten designers, engineers, researchers, architects, and advocates to articulate seven (7) key ideas behind the concept of "universal design." (In the interests of full disclosure: The author of this book is on the Center's advisory board.) The team included the late Ronald L. Mace, who was then the CUD executive director; Molly Story, a product designer and a member of CUD's Design Development team, in Denver, CO; Mike Jones, then CUD co-director and now at the Shepherd Spinal Center, Atlanta, GA; Jim Mueller, president, J. L. Mueller Inc., of Chantilly, VA; Jon Sanford, a specialist in housing and a member of CUD's Research staff, in Atlanta, GA; Bettye Rose Connell, now of the Veterans Administration, Decatur, GA; Elaine Ostroff, then executive director of Adaptive Environments, in Boston, MA (she has since retired but remains a member of its board of directors); Gregg Vanderheiden, professor of human factors and director of the Trace R&D Center, University of Wisconsin at Madison; Ed Steinfeld, Arch.D, director of the Center for Inclusive Design & Environmental Access (IDEA), School of Architecture and Planning, State University of New York at Buffalo; and Abir Mullick, also of the IDEA Center in Buffalo. The team's work was reviewed by another group, this one comprised of eleven educators and practitioners (Story and Mueller, 1998). The principles were formally presented to architects, designers, engineers, and educators at the "Designing for the 21st Century" conference, held June 18–21, 1998, at Hofstra University.

The ways these principles apply to architecture and design are beyond the scope of this book. Readers interested in such applications may learn more from two sources in particular. "Computer Aided Instruction" is a multimedia computer based instructional program that illustrates each of the seven principles of universal design. Case studies exemplify product design, interior design and architecture. This is a Windows-based program. It requires 8 MB of RAM memory, 10 MB of hard-drive space, 16-bit graphics, and at least an Intel 80486 processor. The program is distributed on 3.5 inch disks. "Designing Accessible Environments" is another multimedia instructional program from the IDEA Center. This one offers data on human factors and anthropometrics—which I personally know to be a strength of the Center, because when I was research director for the U.S. Architectural and Transportation Barriers Compliance Board, I funded some of that research. Included are site design, doors and ramps, kitchens, bathrooms, etc. This program, like the other one, is distributed on 3.5" disks and requires the user to have an Intel 80486 processor (or more, such as a Pentium), at least 10 MB of hard-drive space, 8 MB of free memory, and 16-bit graphics. Both are available from the IDEA Center, School of Architecture and Planning, SUNY-Buffalo, Buffalo, NY 14214–3087 or at *www.ap.buffalo.edu/~idea*.

Although the focus of the seven principles was upon architecture, design of consumer products, and engineering, the ideas have meaning for education. This book uses these concepts as a basis for articulating how teachers may provide a universally designed education for their students, whether at elementary and secondary schools or at colleges and universities.

What is universal design? One definition, proposed by Ron Mace and others (1997), reads, "The design of products and environments to be usable by all people, to the greatest extent possible, without the need for adaptation or specialized design." Ron Mace was careful to emphasize that universal design, done properly, benefits all kinds of people. This is a major conceptual break from the traditions of assistive technology. The change traces to recognition, by Mace and Vanderheiden in particular, that people can encounter problems in their environments for reasons related to the circumstances in which they find themselves; those problems are not qualitatively different from similar problems that people with disabilities face because of their impairments. This idea, seemingly simple, turns out to have very significant implications.

Let me make that concrete. Vinton Cerf was one of the originators of what is today known as the Internet. Cerf has been hard-of-hearing all his life; he married a woman who was also hard-of-hearing. For these reasons, when Cerf was playing with the protocols of the ARPANET (the precursor of today's Internet), he plugged in one that allowed for text messaging, so he could communicate with his wife. That was as early as 1972. In the 1990s, as e-mail captured the imaginations of hundreds of millions of people around the world, colleagues of Cerf's (and of mine) whose hearing is perfectly within normal ranges not only accepted this text messaging technology but actually showed a preference for it over voice telephony. Dr. Vanderheiden told me that on a typical day he receives in excess of 150 unique e-mail messages; that is a big multiple over the relatively modest number of voice messages he gets daily. Dr. Vanderheiden has unimpaired hearing, as do the vast majority of his e-mail messengers. This is just one example among many of how a change in the environment, made so as to help people with special needs, unexpectedly turns out to help far greater numbers of individuals with no such needs. Another familiar example: curb cuts. Originally put at intersections so that people using wheelchairs could easily cross streets, curb cuts have proven to be a boon to mothers pushing baby strollers, bicyclists, and many others.

Notice, too, the caveat in Ron Mace's definition that people who have special needs should not be expected to alter products or environments. This immediately raises a question: How does universal design differ from such alterations, notably from assistive technology devices and services, which are commonly used for such adjustments? In general, assistive technology devices and services are used on an after-the-fact basis, when someone with special needs discovers that he or she cannot use a given product or service. To answer the question more fully, let us define the key terms.

DEFINITIONS

A number of definitions have been advanced for the term "universal design." Perhaps the most intriguing is the definition found in the Assistive Technology Act (ATA) of 1998 (PL 105-394). This is because the lawmaking process that led to this Act included a consensus-building exercise in which competing definitions were entertained. The result became definition number 17 in section 3 at the beginning of the Act:

> The term "universal design" means a concept or philosophy for designing and delivering products and services that are usable by people with the widest possible range of functional capabilities, which include products and services that are directly usable (without requiring assistive technologies) and products and services that are made usable with assistive technologies.

Notice, about the ATA definition, that it is consistent with our discussion here: one big advantage of universal design is that it minimizes the need, on the part of people with disabilities, for assistive technology devices and services. The idea is to help people deal with environments they otherwise would find to be hostile (Pirkl, 1994). Still, as the definition acknowledges, universal design will not meet all needs of all people—some persons will still find some environments to be hostile and so will need assistive technology products and services. That is why universally designed products and services must also be compatible with widely used adaptive equipment. In PL 105-394's findings and purposes (section 2), the following explanation appears as statement 10:

> The use of universal design principles reduces the need for many specific kinds of assistive technology devices and assistive technology services by building in accommodations for individuals with disabilities before rather

than after production. The use of universal design principles also increases the likelihood that products (including services) will be compatible with existing assistive technologies. These principles are increasingly important to enhance access to information technology, telecommunications, transportation, physical structures, and consumer products.

I must hasten to add that nothing in the 1998 ATA requires educators or others to practice universal design as the concept is discussed in this book. The term was included in PL 105-394 because the ATA sought to raise awareness about universal design, not because it intended to regulate the design of products and services. Federal grants to state governments are authorized to be used for, among other things, applying the principles of universal design to state-constructed buildings, state-conducted programs and activities, and state-funded services such as transportation; other federal grants are authorized for universities to conduct research about universal design.

The same law (PL 105-394) defines "assistive technology" in definition 2 as "technology designed to be utilized in an assistive technology device or assistive technology service." This, of course, begs the question of how those latter terms are defined. Definition 3 defines "assistive technology device" as "any item, piece of equipment, or product system, whether acquired commercially modified, or customized, that is used to increase, maintain, or improve functional capabilities of individuals with disabilities." Similarly, definition 4 defines "assistive technology service" as, "any service that directly assists an individual with a disability in the selection, acquisition, or use of an assistive technology device. Such term includes [purchasing, leasing, choosing, designing, repairing, etc., assistive technology devices]."

Dr. Vanderheiden and his colleagues at the University of Wisconsin's Trace Center have proposed a definition of universal design ("Principles of Universal Design," at *www.trace.wisc.edu/world*):

The process of designing products, environments, and systems so that they are usable by people with the widest possible range of abilities and circumstances given current technological and commercial constraints. This includes: 1. Designing the products, environments, and systems so that they are directly usable by individuals without requiring any additional assistive devices or adaptations; and 2. Designing the products, environments, and systems so that they can be used with special assistive technologies or adaptations (for those individuals for whom we do not yet know how to provide effective direct accessibility/usability).

Notice, in this definition, that Dr. Vanderheiden places the responsibility for shortcomings in universal design upon the designers and providers of products and services, not upon users. This reminds me of the late Marc Gold, an expert on teaching children with mental retardation. Dr. Gold insisted that if people who are mentally retarded did not learn something, it was because we did not know how to teach it. He developed what he called "Try Another Way," an approach that stressed the use of "task analysis," or the breaking down of tasks into components, and the teaching of those components one by one until the entire task was mastered. That is strikingly parallel to what Dr. Vanderheiden is proposing be done with technological products and services. If a product or service is not usable by some individual, it is the responsibility of its developers to find ways to make it usable, or, at minimum, to arrange for it to be used together with assistive technologies of the user's choice.

The Telecommunications Act of 1996 (PL 104-104) similarly requires that certain new telecommunications products and services be designed to be accessible to people with disabilities, if readily achievable (that is, doable at reasonable cost). If accessibility is not feasible, these products and services must be designed so as to be compatible with popular adaptive products such as Teletypewriters (TTYs), also called Telecommunications Devices for the Deaf (TDDs). This law is specific to telephones and telephone-related products and such services as call waiting, speed dialing, caller identification, and repeat dialing. Those products and services are generally beyond the scope of this text. However, the approach is not. The Act asks manufacturers and service providers to engage in a continuing process of review, recognizing (as does Dr. Vanderheiden) that what is not technically doable today may be tomorrow. The Trace definition calls our attention to the fact that universal design is a process, not an outcome. The Telecommunications Act envisions usability of products and services to be an ongoing process, as well.

I have mentioned that Act several times. Before I leave this topic, allow me to make a parenthetical comment of importance to K–12 schools. PL 104-104 is the source of the very sizeable amounts of money that schools have been using over the past several years to wire schools and classrooms. One provision of the Act, sponsored by United States Senators Olympia Snowe (R,ME) and Jay Rockefeller (D,WV)—for which reason it is sometimes called the "Snowe-Rockefeller amendment" although it is more popularly known as "E-rate"—has channeled billions of dollars to public schools and libraries, especially in rural areas. Its official name is the Universal Service Fund for Schools and Libraries. It provides discounts, ranging from 20% to 90%, off the costs of telecommunications products and services, notably including Internet access and network wiring within school and library buildings. (The greater the poverty of the local area, the higher the discount.) The program is administered by the Schools and Libraries Division (SLD) of the Universal Service Administrative Company (USAC), which was created for this purpose by the Federal Communications Commission (FCC), using its authority under PL 104-104. Schools and libraries were to use these funds for "telecommunications," but they were successful in adopting a broad interpretation of that term. The result has been a tremendous surge of fiber optic and other wiring within the nation's public schools. That wiring has now brought the Internet to most American K–12 students. For more information about the Telecommunications Act, see *www.fcc.gov/dtf*.

Now that the words have been defined, let us make the distinction. Universal design alters the environment and information; assistive technology devices and services let the individual adjust to an unaltered environment or information source. Stated a little differently, in universal design, the burden of changing things rests with the designers and providers of the environment and the information, whereas in assistive technology, the burden rests with the users (with help, as appropriate, from professional engineers, etc.). Universal design makes products and services usable by many people, again and again; a video, once captioned, can be enjoyed by people many times. Assistive technology, by contrast, tends to produce consumable results: an interpreter signs a lecture and once she walks out of the room, the access walks out with her, consumed and non-reusable.

A good illustration of the difference between assistive technology and universal design is offered by closed captioning: prior to the early 1990s, people who wanted captions had to buy $200 caption decoder boxes that sit on top of TV sets; after PL 101-431, the Television Decoder Circuitry Act of 1990, took effect in the mid-1990s, manufacturers built into their commercial TV sets the ability to receive and display captions. That capability, provided by means of a computer chip, cost the manufacturers approximately 25 cents. The black-box decoder was an example of an assistive technology device; the computer chip, by contrast, is an example of universal design. With commercial TV sets sold as caption-ready, captioning found unexpected uses. As one of the authors of PL 101-431, I never did intend for the legislation to benefit staff members on Capitol Hill. Yet, within two years of its enactment, those staff members were among the first beneficiaries: they kept the volume of office TVs off, but the captions on, so they could follow floor debates in Congress while making and receiving phone calls. Captioning is now routinely used in bars and other noisy environments such as airport waiting areas. Senator Tom Harkin (D,IA), who introduced the legislation at my request, told me he uses captioning when someone calls him on the phone, interrupting his enjoyment of a favorite television program. With captioning, he can surreptitiously continue to watch TV while ostensibly giving his full attention to the caller. (I hope the Senator will forgive me for divulging this secret.)

The benefits of universal design, as contrasted with assistive technology, become apparent when costs are considered: products or services designed and marketed specifically for people with disabilities generally carry high costs (often very high!) simply because the potential market is small. To appreciate this, one needs to focus upon specific cases. There is a product that allows people with severe physical disabilities to speak out commands that the house will "obey": one may, for example, say, "Turn on the lights." This product, including its various components, costs as much as a luxury automobile; just the transmitter runs $5,000. Contrast to this the ability of this same person to speak to a PC, saying, for example: "Highlight that paragraph. Now bold it." Cost? About $50 to $75. Why the dramatic difference? Because the latter products, including Dragon Systems' Naturally Speaking™ and IBM's Via Voice™, are marketed to the general population. Because sales volume is so high, development, manufacturing, and other costs may be spread thinly over a great many sales. (Now that I have introduced and named some high-tech products, let me offer a disclaimer. In the 1990s and early in the new century, high technology has evolved at such a rapid pace that products that I name and discuss here quite possibly will not even be sold by the time you read this. The likelihood is, however, that the manufacturers of these technologies will still be marketing something quite similar to the products and services that I describe here. The "Resources" section of this book will help you find the newer versions.)

There are really only two (2) kinds of solutions to the chicken-and-the-egg problem of the high cost of assistive technology. One is for the federal government to guarantee manufacturers of special products that a certain number of devices will be purchased; assured of a sizeable market, the manufacturer can build, and price, on a mass-market scale. This is much like what the federal government did for Chrysler (now DaimlerChrysler) in the early 1980s: it offered a federal guarantee to the then-all-but-bankrupt car maker. Allow me to illustrate with a personal example: a few years ago, I walked the corridors of Congress with the creator of the EyeTyper™, a product allowing people with very severe mobility limitations to type memos and other notes simply by looking at a PC screen. (The device uses a small camera which is focused on the user's eyes; software translates eye movements as the user glances at a "keyboard" on the PC screen to commands that the PC interprets exactly as it interprets key depressions on a keyboard.) He told me that he had sold about 150 of these devices over the past five years, at an average cost of about $35,000 each. The cost is now about $16,000. It could fall even more. Suppose that the federal government guaranteed him that 1,000 of his products would be purchased: the result would be that he could cut the cost of each unit, perhaps to as little as $2,000 (in late 1998, staff members at NASA's Jet Propulsion Laboratory said they had developed a prototype for a similar product which might cost one-tenth the then-price of the EyeTyper™).

The other solution, which does not involve governmental intervention, is universal design. When a product appeals to, and is marketed to, the general population, the price per unit rapidly falls. That is because the benefits of the technology are provided to large swaths of the population, not just to a small group of people having special needs. The product thus sells in the millions of units, not in hundreds. The most obvious illustration of this effect is the personal computer. My first desktop computer cost me nearly $6,000. This was at a time when such machines were used primarily by scientists and research-ers. Today, of course, PCs are used by virtually everybody—I have even seen them in first-grade classrooms. That is why I can now purchase, for less than

$1,000, a desktop machine that is vastly more powerful than the one that cost me six times as much nearly 20 years ago. The distinction between universal design and assistive technology is illustrated in Table 2.1.

THE SEVEN PRINCIPLES

In this chapter, the principles are introduced. Chapter 3 applies them to education. Chapter 4 discusses the first two principles in depth. Chapter 5 then does the same for Principles Three and Four. In Chapter 6, two more principles are discussed in detail (Principles Five and Six). Chapter 7 discusses the final principle (Principle Seven), which applies primarily to buildings and classroom facilities. In Chapter 8, issues related to the World Wide Web are discussed, because of its growing importance in education.

Each principle has a number and a name (e.g., "Principle One: Equitable Use"). Following the name is a brief "definition." Several "guidelines" that spell out how the principle should be applied then follow. This chapter adopts the exact words of the principles, descriptions, and guidelines as copyrighted by CUD. The Center should be credited as the source for this wording and for these principles. Major funding for the development of the ideas was provided by the U.S. Department of Education, National Institute on Disability and Rehabilitation Research (NIDRR); this federal funding makes the ideas public domain, but credit should still be given to the Center as the originator of the principles and as the author of their exact wording.

Table 2.1
Universal Design v. Assistive Technology

Universal Design	Assistive Technology
Responsibility of designers/developers	Responsibility of user or user's agent
Done while service or product is being developed	Done after product is finished, or while service is being delivered
Serves many people at once	Serves one individual user at a time
Renewable accessibility	Consumable accessibility
Allows for serendipity	Seldom is used in innovative ways

Principle One: Equitable Use

Definition: The design is useful and marketable to people with diverse abilities.

As one might expect, with the term "universal design" being intended by Ron Mace and others to play a marketing role, the first principle targets marketing. The general idea is to try to make features that are necessary for people with disabilities attractive to people without disabilities.

Guideline 1a: Provide the same means of use for all users: identical whenever possible; equivalent when not.

An excellent example of this principle at work is Nokia's[R] 9110 cellular phone. At the time this book was written, the product was only available in Europe, where it was selling for about $600. Nokia[R] plans to introduce a version of this phone in the United States and in Japan in late 2000. What is interesting about this phone is that it is one of only a handful (pun intended) of cell phones that are usable both by deaf and by hearing people. People who cannot hear well enough to use the phone in the traditional manner (speaking and listening) can use it to exchange e-mail-like text messages, e-mail, and faxes. They can even transmit photos. To understand the very positive aspects of this phone, consider that people who are deaf pay almost as much (nearly $500) for TTYs that are far more limited in use. TTYs are also perceived by many people who became deaf later in life as "stigmatizing" and thus are shunned. The Nokia[R] phone, by contrast, is not only not seen as non-stigmatizing but it is actually thought of as "cool" because of its popularity among young adults. In addition, the Nokia[R] 9110[tm] is a mainstream product, which means that its price will fall over time. (Details: *www.nokia.com.*)

At Hofstra University, large buses known as "Blue Beetles" traverse the north and south campuses and connect to the local Long Island Rail Road station and to nearby shopping centers. Of the five buses, three have lifts for wheelchair users. Although the university would like to provide lifts on all buses, that will not occur for several more years because it would require buying new buses. Even with only three buses equipped with lifts, accessible bus service is made available to people on an "equivalent" basis because the Beetles follow each other at about 15-minute intervals; the wait is never very long. Ambulatory passengers use all five buses. That adheres to this guideline.

Sometimes, following Guideline 1a causes problems. As an example, consider wide, grab-bar-equipped, stalls in rest rooms. These big stalls are popular, especially in women's rest rooms. They may be used (and should be) by ambulatory persons. Many such individuals, however, are reluctant to use those stalls. They have been confused by the prominence of "handicapped" parking spaces in parking lots; those spaces are reserved for the use of people who have wheelchairs or use other mobility devices. Thus, the hesitation: in bathrooms, the "handicapped" symbol does not say, "For exclusive use of people with physical and mobility limitations," but in parking lots, the same symbol does say that. At Hofstra, we regard this confusion as an acceptable side-effect of an otherwise appropriate policy on facility use. (I would, however, welcome suggestions on resolving it: *frank.bowe@hofstra.edu* .)

Guideline 1b: Avoid segregating or stigmatizing any users.

We follow this guideline when we make the main entrances of buildings universally usable; we violate it if we make back or side entrances, but not the main ones, accessible. Another example of this: The NCR Corporation, spun off a few years ago by AT&T, introduced in Summer 1999 a cash transaction machine known as "Stella"^{tm}. Bank customers begin interacting with Stella^{tm} by stepping onto a pad; this positions them at the right distance for Stella^{tm} to recognize them by "reading" their iris patterns. Stella^{tm} then greets them by speaking their name and asking how "she" can help. Customers interact with the machine by talking; Stella^{tm} "listens" via speech-recognition software. There is no screen to be read, no card slot to be used, and no Personal Identification Number (PIN) to be remembered and entered. Stella^{tm} "knows" a bank's customers better than most live tellers do. In fact, Stella^{tm}, knowing that this customer regularly withdraws $100 before a weekend, might even ask, "Do you want the usual?" NCR plans to experiment with the design, perhaps changing it, and then to roll it out worldwide ("New Girl in Town," July 16, 1999, *www.atmmagazine.com*). What is nice about this is that it offers banking services to customers who are blind at the same locations as services are rendered to sighted customers: blind customers are not segregated. In late 1999, Citibank installed talking ATM's in five California branches. These machines combine touch screens with speech synthesis. Users hear on-screen information through headphones. Don Brown, president of the California Council of the Blind, a chapter of the American Council of the Blind (ACB), praised the new devices: "Citibank's machine is tremendous— it allows me for the first time to do a variety of banking transactions unassisted." (For information,e-mail: lfeingold@california.net.)

Guideline 1c: Make provisions for privacy, security, and safety equally available to all users.

To continue with the Citibank example, it is important that customers have access to headphones to listen to the computer-generated voice; otherwise, of course, nearby customers would overhear balance data and other private information. This security measure serves sighted as well as blind customers. At Hofstra, campus security personnel offer to escort students from classroom buildings to their cars during evening hours, when requested, despite the fact that robberies and assaults have been rare on the campus in recent years.

Guideline 1d: Make the design appealing to all users.

Accessibility will be accepted by the general public only if it is attractive. Costs will fall only if such acceptance occurs. Accordingly, wide appeal is a critical element of universal design. Again, Stella[tm] and the Citibank ATM's illustrate: a "hearing" and "talking" ATM will be used by bank customers only if they find it comfortable and appealing. If they do not, bank customers who are blind or have dyslexia will find such machines at few if any banks. Why are Nokia[R] cell phones the world's top selling models? Because they appeal to us with large, very easy-to-read screens (significantly bigger and clearer than are the competitions'), color (you can switch the front covers to make the phone red, blue, silver, etc.), logical key layouts (keys do what one intuitively expects them to do), and other user-friendly features. Why are La-Z-Boy[tm] chairs so popular with Baby Boomers? Because they are big, comfortable, and come equipped with convenient cup holders—all of which respond to the desires of 50-ish Boomers who are a few pounds heavier than they would like to be, who welcome the "give" of the cushions, and who return home from a hectic workday and relish the chairs' reclining features, which are conducive to much-anticipated naps.

Principle Two: Flexibility in Use
Definition: The design accommodates a wide range of individual preferences and abilities.

If universal design is to appeal to the general public, it must meet the needs of a broad variety of people, from very young children to very large men to very old women. Doing this is a challenge even for industrial designers trained in meeting different needs. For many years, designers have been taught in school to configure products so as to be useable by the vast middle "90%" and to ignore the "5%" at each tail. That, as it turns out, is exactly the problem. The real change posed by universal design is that it tells them to incorporate those tails as well.

Guideline 2a: Provide choices in methods of use.

An example illustrating this is the "Talking Caller ID"[tm] box. Bell Atlantic, the regional Bell operating company providing local, wireless, and other phone services in the northeast region (Maine to Virginia) offers its customers the opportunity to buy Caller ID service and to receive a Caller ID box. The service displays, on the box's screen, the number and/or the name of the calling party; this allows Bell Atlantic customers to see who is calling before they answer, giving them the option of answering or not. The Talking Caller ID[tm] box also "speaks" out loud the calling party's number and/or name. For most Bell Atlantic customers, this is a convenience—they need not get up and rush to the phone to read the screen, but can simply listen, from wherever they happen to be. For customers who are blind or who have certain learning disabilities, however, the "talking" feature makes the Caller ID service accessible. They can use it— they could not without this feature. (Details: *www.bellatlantic.com*). In late June, 2000, Bell Atlantic merged with GTE to form Verizon Communications.

Guideline 2b: Accommodate right- or left-handed access and use.

The classic example of a violation of this rule is the telephone booth. (A rarity these days!) They were very difficult for left-handed people to use. In classrooms, the vast majority of student desk are right-handed models. One solution to this problem is for the teacher or students to scavenge desks from other rooms so as to bring in enough left-handed desks. A better one: design a student desk that can be "flipped" from a right- to a left-handed configuration.

Guideline 2c: Facilitate the user's accuracy and precision.

This guideline is most readily appreciated with respect to consumer-use products like cell phones, pocket calculators, et cetera: they have gotten so small in size that the keys are tiny and tightly compressed. At some point, those keys are simply too small and too close together. People will reject such products, because they lead to too many errors and because they are uncomfortable to use. Another, more obscure, example: people with cerebral palsy often use "key guards"—plastic boards that fit over computer keyboards and feature holes above keys. The main purpose of the key guards is to guide the user's finger toward the correct key. However, there is a second, rather unintended effect: the plastic board provides a resting place for the user's hands, thus allowing them to brace themselves, stabilize their hands and fingers, and then type. (I thank Dr. Vanderheiden for offering this example: as someone who has devoted his entire working career to technology for people with cerebral palsy and other disabilities, he was among the first to notice this unexpected benefit.)

Guideline 2d: Provide adaptability to the user's pace.

Voice-mail systems frequently violate this principle. They present options too rapidly and fail to allow users to adjust the pace. Elevator call systems sometimes break this rule, too. Fortunately, in recent years, elevator bank lights flash on several seconds before an elevator arrives, thus giving people time to position themselves in front of the appropriate elevator shaft.

Principle Three: Simple and Intuitive Use

Definition: Use of the design is easy to understand, regardless of the user's experience, knowledge, language skills, or current concentration level.

Principle Three is most directly applicable to consumer and office-use products such as PCs, ATMs, and other devices we use daily. It has become very important in the 1990s. To illustrate, e-mail addresses at Hofstra University were created, in the early years of the decade, by people at the Academic Computing Center, that is, by computer types. They decided that faculty members would have addresses comprised of three letters from the academic department name plus three initials (meaning my e-mail address became *serfgb@hofstra.edu,* for Special Education and Rehabilitation, Frank G. Bowe). The only problem was that people from around the country and for that matter the world who knew me and wanted to e-mail me generally did not know my academic department; that the department name changed in the early 1990s did not help. Only in 1999 were professors finally able to bring some real-world intuition to the process: we insisted that our e-mail addresses be our first and last names, separated by a period (mine is *frank.bowe@hofstra.edu*). People can remember and accurately type this address much better. (Trace's Vanderheiden e-mailed me shortly after the change: "I always wondered what on earth your e-mail address used to stand for!")

Guideline 3a: Eliminate unnecessary complexity.

As an example, Bell Atlantic (now Verizon) offers VoiceDialing™. In this service, the customer simply speaks the name of the person or company and the service automatically dials that person's or company's number. This is a convenience for most customers. But for people who have cerebral palsy, quadriplegia, severe arthritis, or other fine-motor-control limitations, the service makes it possible for them to "dial" phone numbers with ease. For other customers, including some who are mentally retarded and some who have certain learning disabilities, the service makes it possible for them to "dial" the correct number. (Many people with learning disabilities mis-dial numbers because they mix up the order of the digits.)

Guideline 3b: Be consistent with user expectations and intuition.

To continue with telephone analogies, consider name- and acronym-based phone numbers (i.e., 1-800-FLOWERS). These are easy to remember. However, the human factors turn out to be bad: actually dialing such numbers is painfully slow, because we are not accustomed to dialing by letter. Another example: In my home, we have a hair dryer that inexplicably has the "off" setting as the middle of three vertically set levels; the top level is "low" and the bottom level is "high." I have to look at the settings each time I use this hair dryer, which is annoying. A third example: user manuals for computer hardware and software. When I don't know how to do something, the last thing I try is to look into the user manual. These tend to be written for the kinds of people who wrote them: computer professionals. Few and far between are manuals that actually anticipate user problems and answer those, up front and quickly.

Guideline 3c: Accommodate a wide range of literacy and language skills.

In the Introduction and Executive Summary, I gave the example of user manuals for Hewlett Packard printers. These manuals rely more on drawings than on text. The entire manual for some models is a single folded sheet of paper. These manuals make changing print cartridges, cleaning the printer, et cetera, easy and trouble-free. When I shop for a new computer printer, I buy Hewlett-Packard printers, even when a competing maker offers a less expensive model having more features. That is how important clear directions are, even for me, a Ph.D. with well-developed reading skills.

Guideline 3d: Arrange information consistent with its importance.

Think about the last time you visited a large facility and used a building map (or, as we have at Hofstra, a campus map). If you're like me, you look first for some visual indicator of where you are ("You Are Here!"). I like it much better when maps highlight my position, so I can identify it in seconds. I also benefit from maps which highlight important landmarks that are visible from my location. Those help me to orient myself, that is, to compare what I see on the map to what I see around me. Hofstra's campus maps do that. By contrast, maps that do not provide highlighting for important items can be unnecessarily confusing. A few weeks ago, needing to ship an overnight package to Tokyo, I drove into JFK International Airport, in New York City, in search of the Japan Air Lines Cargo facility. After half an hour of fruitless searching, I accidentally came across the airport map. Even after finding it, it took ten full minutes to locate the indicator for Building 171 on the map— and even then, I wasn't quite sure where the building actually stood in that very large airport. Making matters worse is that the numbering of buildings at JFK bears no relationship to their locations: Building 171 is adjacent to Building 85, but a good mile from Building 170.

A related principle in this guideline is: Provide effective prompting and feedback during and after task completion. As you can see from my example of Hofstra's campus maps, the "You Are Here" prompt gets me started and prominent highlights of nearby buildings give me feedback.

Guideline 3e: Provide effective prompting and feedback during and after task completion.

This guideline warns us away from membrane keyboards. Most membranes are flat—they provide no tactile confirmation and sound no "click" to tell the user that he or she has successfully pressed the key. They are often impossible for people who are blind to use. Some membranes have a lip and do offer a minimal tactile feedback, for which reason these could be used by people who are blind, but those are few and far between.

Principle Four: Perceptible Information
Definition: The design communicates necessary information effectively to the user, regardless of ambient conditions or the user's sensory abilities.

This is an excellent guideline for explaining why people with no disabilities should care about accessible features. While most people have hearing that functions very well, there are times when it does not. Conversation in my neighborhood ceases each time a jet passes overhead, bound for or departing from the nearby JFK. People standing on subway stations cannot hear on unamplified phones. When lights go out, everyone temporarily becomes "blind." Another example: if I am typing a manuscript like this one, I cannot simultaneously keep my eye on a Penn State football game. People who hear have no problem—they can simply listen to the broadcast of the Nittany Lions game while typing. Fortunately for sports fans, AOL offers a neat feature where the scores of ongoing games, updated every few minutes, are displayed in a small box in one corner of the screen.

Guideline 4a: Use different modes (pictorial, verbal, tactile) for redundant presentation of essential information.

Redundancy means, as I suggested earlier, that information that a product, service, or teacher presents aurally should also be offered visually, and vice versa. At train stations and within train cars and buses, stops and destinations should be announced both ways. Friends of mine who are blind constantly complain about television commercials that intone: "Call the number on your screen!" without enunciating that number; they have no idea what number to dial.

As a person who is deaf, I find very frustrating auditory-only communication systems in buildings. An auxiliary building of Hofstra's library, for example, permits entry from the street level only for people who are "buzzed in" after pushing a doorbell. There is no way I can even know whether I have reached someone inside after pushing the button, let alone what that person says to me. That's why I really like the new Honeywell Video Entry System™. It lets apartment dwellers or office workers see visitors, and vice versa. The addition of a visual communication mode makes all the difference for people who cannot hear. (Details: *www.honeywell.com* or 1-800-345-6770, ext. 2008.)

Guideline 4b: Maximize "legibility" of essential information.

Interestingly, the first draft of this guideline emphasized the importance of distinguishing important words and symbols from surrounding walls and other environments. Ron Mace and his colleagues later changed the guideline's description, placing quotation marks around the word "legibility" to suggest that what they had in mind was not only readability by people who cannot read print, but aural and tactile contrast, as well. A good example of this concept in use is bathroom signs that display both a human figure and the words "Men" or "Women" in type.

Guideline 4c: Differentiate elements in ways that can be described (i.e., make it easy to give instructions or directions).

Again, Ron and his collaborators were concerned that simple highlighting or colorizing of elements on a map, or other important symbols, would not make it easy for sighted people to describe those to persons who are blind. But the idea also applies to other uses. One is for buttons on a TV or a VCR to be shaped differently; that way, I could tell a visitor who is blind, "Just touch the square button on the top edge." User manuals and customer–service staff members should also follow this guideline.

Guideline 4d: Provide compatibility with a variety of techniques or devices used by people with sensory limitations.

When the Telecommunications Act of 1996 (PL 104-104) required, in section 255, that new telecommunications products be accessible to people with disabilities, Congress was careful to qualify the new mandate with the words "insofar as readily achievable." That is, if making them accessible was not easily doable, manufacturers did not have to do so. However, this did not let them off the hook. They were required to ensure that their products were compatible with (worked well together with) the assistive technology devices that people with disabilities use, such as TTYs.

Principle Five: Tolerance for Error

Definition: The design minimizes hazards and the adverse consequences of accidental or unintended actions.

This principle is an important one because of the way we live our lives today. We use so many products, most of them electronic, that Ron Mace and his colleagues had to include a principle like this one. When I set the house alarm before leaving for work, I am always a little tense. There is a beep that the alarm system emits if I were to omit an essential step and accidentally set off the alarm, but being deaf I don't hear those beeps. There have been occasions (fortunately few in number) when I have driven off only to be told later that the local police responded to a false alarm at my house. The systems offered by our local security firms do not tolerate the kinds of errors I sometimes make.

Guideline 5a: Arrange elements to minimize hazards and errors: most used elements, most accessible; hazardous elements eliminated, isolated, or shielded.

Xerox copiers and printers excel on this (in the interests of full disclosure, I was a consultant for Xerox in the 1980s on machines that used these features for the first time). When you open a Xerox printer or copier, the inside controls that are intended for human use (and that are safe for users to operate) are green; those that users should not touch are red or dark orange. This use of colors quickly guides the eye to the levers that you need to manipulate in order to clear a paper jam or perform other routine maintenance on the machine and away from levers you should not touch.

Guideline 5b: Provide warnings of hazards and errors.

This guideline is important at the turn of the century because we use so many machines in our daily lives, and some of them could be dangerous if not operated properly. As critical as warnings are, they should be user-comprehensible. Microsoft's early messages of impending operating-system crashes ("Fatal 404 Error") induced unnecessary anxiety in users. In the late 1990s, Microsoft softened and clarified the messages.

Guideline 5c: Provide fail–safe features.

The original draft of this guideline read: "Make input reversible." That is a fail-safe feature that people need in more software programs. One of my greatest frustrations with the "remote access" software implementing the e-mail system Hofstra adopted traces from the fact that when the system freezes, there is no way to recover except to shut down the PC. Another example of this guideline in action: the dealer that leases me the car I drive every day gave me a thin leather folder containing an extra key. It fits into my wallet. That way, were I to lock myself out of the car, I can still open it. A third example, one also showing that being a university professor was a good career move for me: I have on occasion started heating up a coffee pot without verifying that the pot actually contained water. Some of the newer stoves will automatically shut off a burner if the pot becomes too hot. (This fact makes getting a new stove one of my priorities for the house.)

Guideline 5d: Discourage unconscious action in tasks that require vigilance.

Ron Mace and his colleagues recognized reality: all of us become tired at one point or another. We are all also creatures of habit. For these reasons, we occasionally need a reminder. Some computer software programs require users to confirm key information. For example, when you are prompted to enter a password, the program demands that you re-type that password for confirmation. Similarly, Windows 98[R] will not allow you to shut down the computer without first asking if you are "sure" that this is your intent. Another example: Nokia's[R] newer cell phones shield the keys when the phone is stored in a pocket or pocketbook. This shielding is important: people using other makes of cell phones occasionally have been embarrassed when the one-button dial feature was accidentally activated from within a pocket or pocketbook and their supposedly private conversations were transmitted to family or co-workers!

Principle Six: Low Physical Effort
Definition: The design can be used efficiently and comfortably and with a minimum of fatigue.

This principle responds to the needs of many ambulatory but elderly citizens. It also respects reality with regard to young children. These features help universal design to become universally appealing.

Guideline 6a: Allow user to maintain a neutral body position.

The design of automobiles in the 2000 and 2001 model years illustrates how companies struggle to meet diverse needs. With the huge pig-in-a-python Baby Boom generation entering its 50s, car makers want to appeal to older drivers as never before; yet, at the same time, they want to continue to attract younger, trend-setting customers. Royal Ford, writing in the *Boston Globe*, caught the contradictions in his "Auto Designs for the Ages" story of March 5, 2000. Ford says that the car manufacturers' decisions are those presented in this book: They practice the principles of universal design, making vehicles that are usable both by older and younger drivers, but they *market* these cars differently to different segments of the car-buying population.

Ford quotes Lear Corporation's Karen Stewart-Spica as saying the key is (to use industry jargon) "transparent enablers"—unobtrusive features that meet varying needs. An example is night vision systems. These help older drivers, who tend not to see as well at night. Car salesmen pitch the systems that way to senior shoppers. The same technology, however, is marketed to young drivers as the "newest, coolest" thing, sort of like picture-in-a-picture on TV sets.

Lear itself offers concept vehicle, the TransG (for TransGeneration) van. This van's pedals, steering wheel and dash display all move toward the driver, making them more easily, and more safely, usable by smaller and older persons. The steering wheel is half-moon, like that of an airplane; this makes viewing gauges on the display much easier. Seats swivel 45 degrees, making entrance and egress much more comfortable.

The new Ford Focus (which replaces the Escort) features wide front-door openings at knee level that let drivers swing legs into the car more easily. It also has seats a little higher from street level than did the Escort, again because it takes more effort to rise from a low seat than from a higher one. I can attest to that from personal experience—when I need to drive my daughter's Mustang, emerging from the car is noticeably harder than it is with other vehicles I have driven. Other features found on some new cars include seat belts that clasp in the middle, rather than attaching on one side (it is far easier for older people to clasp at belt level than to twist the body to connect traditional seatbelt buckles); ignitions that are on the dashboard rather than the steering column (twisting the key is easier if the wrist is not already bent); and large controls for radio and other devices (both easier to see and easier to manipulate) (Bradsher, 1999).

"Ergonomic" chairs and keyboards are called that for a reason. Microsoft offers an ergonomic keyboard (the Natural Keyboard Elite[tm], designed by Ziba Design) that costs almost $300 (v. the roughly $10 that ordinary keyboards cost in office supply stores). This keyboard has resting areas for wrists and upper arms, as well as "wells" or cavities for fingers to reach keys. The prices remain stubbornly high because relatively few people have purchased them. Any occupational therapist will tell you that this Microsoft keyboard is well worth the money. Ergonomic chairs, similarly, position the body in ways that help to prevent back injuries (probably the single most common kind of occupational injury in America today) because they allow the body to remain in a comfortable yet natural position.

Guideline 6b: Use reasonable operating forces.

Of course, what is "reasonable" varies depending on who is asked. Doors that young children need to be able to open and close should require much less pressure to operate than doors that only security personnel operate. We at Hofstra have a "Unispan" walking bridge that crosses over a major highway, connecting the north and south campuses. This Unispan, built many years ago, is much too steep for comfortable use by people in manual wheelchairs; it is also a challenge for the food-service workers who traverse the Unispan to deliver catered food to meetings in the south campus. When the University considered adding a second Unispan, plans called for a much less steep vertical slope. Those plans were widely hailed as being user-friendly, both by ambulatory persons and by wheelchair users.

Guideline 6c: Minimize repetitive actions.

Why is carpal tunnel syndrome so common these days? Because workers in some jobs, notably jobs requiring data entry, have to repeat the same motions thousands of times throughout the work day. While each effort is minimal, the sustained nature of those efforts is not: the effect is cumulative. As a professor, I can give myself a break and do very different work (read a term paper, for example), but many office workers do not have that luxury. Managements should restructure those jobs so that, at frequent and predictable times throughout the day, data-entry workers leave their terminals and do very different things.

Guideline 6d: Minimize sustained physical effort.

The intent of this guideline, as the 1995 working draft developed by Ron Mace and his colleagues makes clear, is to minimize user fatigue. The wording was changed, in part because what people consider to be "sustained physical effort" may not be a matter of fatigue at all, but rather one of undue effort. When things are "too hard" to do, people don't want to do them. Maytag Appliances (Newton, Iowa) has been pleasantly surprised by the popularity of its Neptune™ clothes washers. Knowing that front-loading machines would be much more energy efficient than top-loading ones—front-loaders require 50% less electrical energy and 40% less water—but also that people do not like to have to bend to insert clothes into the washers, Maytag tilted the washer's drum upward 15 degrees from horizontal and enlarged the mouth (opening) and thus achieved a happy compromise: a front-loading washer that does not require users to bend at the knee. The results speak for themselves: even though the product is costly (a bit more than $1,000, v. $400 to $500 for top-loading washers), it is a hit because consumers do not need to sacrifice in order to achieve the energy savings front loaders bring ("Great Machines," 1999).

In the late 1970s and early 1980s, General Motors earned my wrath when they placed the wheelchair lifts of their mass-transit buses at the rear rather than at the front. With rear lifts, the bus operator must first turn off the ignition, rise, walk the length of the bus, insert a key into the lift, lower it, then (after the passenger gets on the lift) raise it again, lock the lift, traverse the length of the bus again, and start the ignition again. The foreseeable result is that bus operators resist picking up passengers in wheelchairs. Another outcome: ambulatory passengers sometimes resent the amount of time the operator spends doing these things (as many as ten minutes). GM's competitors in the mass-transit bus market smartly placed the lifts at the front of buses. In those buses, the operator remains seated, and simply (and quickly) operates the lift from where he or she is. The result is a much greater willingness to stop for people using wheelchairs. Another result: other passengers are much more amenable to such stops, knowing that those will be short.

The ultimate in minimized physical effort is automatic doors. We see these frequently now, in airports, in grocery stores, and (at least at Hofstra) in some classroom buildings. If you find yourself with a few minutes on your hands, watch how those doors make life easier for people carrying packages, pushing grocery carts or kiddie strollers, delivering equipment, et cetera, and not just for people using wheelchairs.

Principle Seven: Size and Space for Approach and Use

Definition: Appropriate size and space is provided for approach, reach, manipulation, and use regardless of user's body size, posture, or mobility.

Ever try to change sheets in a convertible bed? Tucking the sheet in at the headboard end is a challenge. (I find I have to kneel on the bed to do it.) Wouldn't it be nice if I could tuck that end in while standing, as I can the other end?

Guideline 7a: Provide a clear line of sight to important elements for any seated or standing user.

A new sports arena was opened in Washington, DC, in 1997. Only then did sports fans discover that the "wheelchair accessible" sites were positioned behind columns that obstructed the views of fans in wheelchairs. It took a lawsuit, filed by Eastern Paralyzed Veterans Association, to move the accessible sites to locations with unobstructed views.

Guideline 7b: Make reach to all components comfortable for any seated or standing user.

Light switches are easily reached while you are standing, but they can be hard to operate while seated; electrical outlets are the opposite. In some universally designed houses and offices, both sets of switches are reachable whether you are seated or standing. With respect to older people in particular, provide chairs that have armrests—these people may well need to push against the arm rests to stand up.

Guideline 7c: Accommodate variations in hand and grip size.

The other day, my wife surprised me by asking me to buy a box of large-grip pens. She's never done that before—but then, we never had FlexGrip^{tm} pens in the house before. She just likes them. Little people like them, too, as do children. The wonder is that it took pen manufacturers until 1998 and 1999 to realize that big-grip implements are comfortable for all of us while, at the same time, responding to variations in grip size. Oxo^R brand kitchen utensils are also good; designed for people who have less grip strength, they also just "feel better" for people with unimpaired grip strength. An example is the Oxo^R Good Grips^{tm} peeler created by Smart Design.

Guideline 7d: Provide adequate space for the use of assistive devices or personal assistance.

The obvious examples are wheelchairs, walkers, and crutches, and, with respect to "personal assistance," human aides and guide dogs. Wheelchair users need knee space under tables as well as writing surfaces that are at writing height. Walkers, crutches, and the like require storage space near the student's or worker's desk, as do guide dogs. Human aides may sit at adjacent desks.

Chapter 3

Universally Designed Education

In education, "universal design" means the preparation of curricula, materials, and environments so that they may be used, appropriately and with ease, by a wide variety of people. Universal design places responsibility for making adjustments upon the instructors and the school. Only students posing unusual special needs are expected to provide their own accommodations. The Council for Exceptional Children (CEC) has offered a definition of universal design in education:

> In terms of learning, universal design means the design of instructional materials and activities that makes the learning goals achievable by individuals with wide differences in their abilities to see, hear, speak, move, read, write, understand English, attend, organize, engage, and remember. Universal design for learning is achieved by means of flexible curricular materials and activities that provide alternatives for students with differing abilities. These alternatives are built into the instructional design and operating systems of educational materials—they are not added on after-the-fact. (*Research Connections*, Number 5, Fall 1999, p. 2)

One recent book, *The Accessible School: Universal Design for Educational Settings* (Bar and Galluzzo, 1999), tells us to think of universal design as applying to the physical environment. That is a part of what "universal design in education" means (see Chapter 7), but it is only a part of it. Laurel Bar and Judith Galluzzo, both occupational therapists, showed in their book how to apply the principles of accessible design to the built environment of public schools and classrooms. While helpful, that information may not assist many educators, because most of us do not have the opportunity to design buildings or classrooms. Rather, we in this text must look at universal design much more broadly—as applied also to what we do inside the built environment.

Universal design in education is based upon the premise that by preparing to meet diverse needs, we will better serve people with no special needs. As a recent report from the National Academy of Sciences (Biermann, 1997) put it:

> [A]iming for use by every citizen can enhance use by ordinary citizens. Eve the seemingly ordinary are heterogeneous: the general population varies greatly in computer skills (e.g., from novice to expert); in the ability to speak, read, and write English; in personal cognitive styles (e.g., from linguistic/verbal to spatial/visual); and in personal propensity for using complex technological gadgets. (Executive Summary, p. 2)

That report, *More Than Screen Deep: Toward Every-Citizen Interfaces to the Nation's Information Infrastructure* (1997), suggested that responding to multiple needs means acting along three (3) dimensions:

* Learnability (ease of learning)
* Modality and medium independence (ease of use), and
* Supporting group activities (interconnectiveness).

Briefly: The "learnability" dimension responds to our recognition that initial adopters of technologies—the kinds of people who "must have" the newest, fastest, coolest computers and other electronic gadgets—are different in many ways from late adopters. Most notably, they adjust quickly and effortlessly to the peculiarities of hardware and software. Initial adopters of what became (much later) the Internet comfortably put up with the oddities of UNIX and the demands of command-line interfaces; late adopters would not and did not. Modality and medium independence means supporting a range of input technologies (including speech recognition, natural language processing, and even computer vision and gesture sensing), output technologies (including speech synthesis, high-resolution and flexible displays, and multimodal generation of output), and nomadicity (the usability of the system wherever the student happens to be; now more commonly called "mobile computing"). The very essence of education in the Internet Age is networking. It is essential that we encourage collaboration. In the words of Nathan Shedroff (1997), writing in the *Screen Deep* report: "People are becoming active audiences and participants instead of merely users. They are increasingly communicating with others and creating meaningful things rather than merely 'viewing' and watching" (p. 5).

Gregg Vanderheiden, one of the nation's most prominent pioneers in shaping technology so as to meet special needs, explored the concept of "nomadicity" in depth for the *Screen Deep* report. Dr. Vanderheiden noted that many people have difficulty hearing, some of whom cannot hear at all. He then went on to note that, at some times and in some locations, people who ordinarily have no difficulty hearing are rendered, for all intents and purposes, hearing-impaired. An example is a commuter waiting at the 42nd Street stop for the "A" train. The arriving and departing subways in this Manhattan subway station make so much noise that people with unimpaired hearing are, temporarily, deaf. They need amplification in order to hear on a phone. This is an example of nomadicity: in our very mobile society, there are times and locales where virtually all of us have special needs. There are other examples, Vanderheiden wrote: times and places when people whose vision is well within normal limits are unable to see, or nearly so; times when people with intelligence that is within the normal range are unable to remember things (i.e., sleep deprivation). For all of these reasons, when designers make educational materials and techniques usable by people with disabilities, they also make them more widely usable by people who have no disabilities.

Consider Biermann's (1997) point that people differ greatly in their abilities to read, to type, and to use complex devices. Vanderheiden observed that by designing machines so as to make them usable by people who are blind or have low vision, notably by making them "talk," we are also easing matters for people who are illiterate or have little functional reading ability as well as for people who have little experience or knowledge in using electronic devices. This is illustrated in the innovative approaches for designing such touchscreen devices as kiosks, automatic teller machines, and the home appliances that the Trace team has developed (see *http://trace.wisc.edu/world/kiosks*). Similarly, the "ShowSounds" feature that Vanderheiden invented to help people who have little or no residual hearing ability can assist people who find themselves in noisy environments. ShowSounds produces visible symbols for sounds, such as warning bells. It is built into Windows^{tm} and Macintosh^{tm} operating systems, such as Mac OS 8.6^{tm} and Mac OS 9.0^{tm}. This technology is also described at the Trace Web site.

People also differ greatly within themselves. I can no longer see as well as I did 40 years ago. Moving one of my daughters into a university dorm room leaves me with muscle aches that take days to go away—aches I didn't even feel when I was their age. Steven Miller made the same point when he noted: "We all need to remember that being among the 'temporarily able-bodied' is a short-term gift" (1996, p. 2). (I hope Steve remembers this himself—he is, as this is written, among the "temporarily able-bodied.")

Students vary—and they vary a lot. We prefer not to think about that too much—we have 25 or more students in a class, and it is just easier to teach somewhere in the middle, hoping that the brighter ones, the ones who have more experience/knowledge, or those who have a natural affinity for the subject will not become bored, and that those who are going to struggle will put in the time on their own and somehow keep pace. It is far better, though, to customize. This means PCs and Web sites. These tools offer incredible opportunities to individualize instruction—and make customizing very easy, very fast.

UNIVERSAL DESIGN IN PREK–12 SCHOOLS

In the United States, public preschools, elementary schools, and high schools are required by federal and state law to provide "a free appropriate public education" for students who have disabilities. The major laws are the Individuals with Disabilities Education Act (IDEA; 20 U.S.C. 1400), the Americans with Disabilities Act (ADA; 42 U.S.C. 12101), and the Rehabilitation Act (29 U.S.C. 706).

PreK–12 teachers can expect to be advised, before children are placed in their classrooms, whether these children have disabilities and, if so, what those disabilities are. A committee in the school district, known as the Individualized Education Program Team (IEP Team), or going by a similar name, such as the Committee on Special Education, will have assembled information about each child, including what the child needs from you. You may secure that information from your building principal or from the IEP Team itself. You should do so. This material is contained in the child's IEP. That document will tell you: (1) the child's "unique needs" or "current educational performance" (how well the child is doing in different areas of study), (2) special education needs (tutoring, additional time in tests, etc.), and (3) related services (interpreters, physical therapy, et cetera).

Once you have read over the IEP, you most likely will have questions. A good person to ask those questions is the district director of special education, who may refer you to specialists (e.g., a teacher of learning-disabled students). In these meetings, you should ask about special education services (who will do the tutoring? when? where?), related services (who will provide them? when? where?), and the like. You may also wish to talk to the child's prior-year teacher. Quite possibly, the child's parents will make an appointment with you to discuss their priorities and concerns. In PreK–12 programs, parents enjoy certain legal rights. They may challenge the IEP Team in mediation, and/or in court, and they quite often do. Usually, these challenges involve interpretation of the word "appropriate" (the parents may want more special services, the IEP Team less). Given that you carry out the school's policy and the IEP Team's decisions, you are not individually and personally liable in such legal proceedings.

As the year proceeds, you should monitor progress carefully. If the child is not keeping pace with classmates, you should ask whether a reassessment by the IEP Team would be appropriate (i.e., if additional tutoring is needed). Only the IEP Team can alter the IEP. If, after any such changes, the child is still not keeping pace, you may need to make a formal request of the IEP Team that the child's placement be reconsidered. You should not take this step until you are confident that all reasonable measures have been taken to ensure success in the current placement.

With respect to students who are members of ethnic and/or racial minority groups, nondiscrimination is the law. Federal and state statutes do not require the formal planning that is mandated for children who have disabilities. Nonetheless, you should familiarize yourself with how "nondiscrimination" is interpreted in your school district. What is the policy, for example, about religious holidays? What is the school's dress code? What kinds of behaviors are not tolerated? All of this information will help you to determine how flexible you can be about responding to student needs and desires and respecting their cultures.

Students with different learning styles and preferences enjoy no special legal protection in the United States. Some learn best by studying alone; others do much better when they work with a partner. Some absorb information most readily through their ears; others do best when reading. Some excel with words; others have to "see it" in person or act it out to understand it. You have considerable flexibility in how you accommodate such diversity. As a teacher, you should consult your supervisor with respect to school policy in this area.

Issues of input and output are very common in K–12 schools. Learning disabilities comprise more than half of all disabilities at this level of education. Children with no disabilities, but with non-dominant learning styles, are still mastering techniques that they will need for success in school and, later, in work and in life: they are still in need of your help in doing so and, often, of some extra time to complete a project. On the other hand, K–12 children are expected to master certain skills, notably including reading and writing in traditional (or near-traditional) ways. This means that even children with dyslexia (a learning disability that interferes with reading) will be required to read as well as they can. Similarly, even children who learn best in activities ("by doing") are expected to demonstrate knowledge in tests that require reading and writing. As a teacher, then, you will need to strike a balance between the child's needs and preferences, on the one hand, and state and district requirements, on the other. The building principal and the IEP Team can give you guidance in ways to do so.

UNIVERSAL DESIGN IN COLLEGES AND UNIVERSITIES

In American higher education, "nondiscrimination" is required on behalf of students with disabilities and students from minority groups. The Individuals with Disabilities Education Act does not apply; rather, the legal standards are those of the Americans with Disabilities Act and the Rehabilitation Act.

Formal plans such as IEPs are not used. Rather, in colleges and universities, the student is required to bring any special needs or preferences to the attention of a college official usually known as a "special services coordinator" (sometimes called a "section 504 coordinator"). This person, often assisted by a staff of specialists, acts at the student's instigation. The difference from K–12 education is stark: if the student does not make a request, no accommodation is even considered by the special services coordinator's office, let alone provided. If the student makes such a request, this office arranges sign language interpreters, tutors, personal-care assistants, etc., to work with the student. As a teacher, you do not need to be involved in this process. The special services coordinator will alert you, possibly in a memo or perhaps in an in-person meeting, about any accommodations that will be made. If you have questions about it, the special services coordinator can answer them.

If the student has not "self identified" (advised the special services coordinator of his or her disability and needs), it is very possible that no record of disability exists anywhere on the campus. Accordingly, if you discover that a student in one of your classes has a severe hearing loss, or some other significant disability, all that you can do is to ask the student (privately, please) if he or she has discussed this with the special services coordinator. If the answer is no, you must accept that answer. You have no right, and no responsibility, to do anything more. Accordingly, the student may fail your course if he or she is not mature enough to accept personal responsibility for the disability. This is, of course, a big difference from K–12 education. In the United States, we treat college students as the adults they are. This is one element of that larger policy.

The college's legal liability, and yours as a professor, ends if the student does not request accommodations. If, on the other hand, the student does ask for an accommodation (say, to take tests in a separate room so as to make effective use of a magnifying device to read the test questions), the responsibility to choose, and implement, the appropriate accommodation rests with the college's special services coordinator, not with you as teacher. Your role is to accept such modifications. (If you object to one or more such adjustments, take the issue up with the special services coordinator.) To refuse to allow such changes would be to subject yourself and the institution to possible legal action.

College and university professors enjoy far more academic freedom than do K–12 teachers. Accordingly, the extent to which you choose to respond to the preferences or desires of students with different learning styles is almost completely up to you. A college student who learns much better through reading than through listening to classroom lectures enjoys no legal protection by virtue of that learning style. As a professor, you can insist upon regular attendance in class, or you can excuse the student from that, or you can require the student to attend some but not all classes. Similarly, the extent to which you respond to differences in behavior and preference on the part of students from minority groups is largely up to you. What you cannot do is to discriminate against any student on the basis of race, ethic group membership, religion, or gender. If you have questions, consult your provost's office.

Learning disabilities which present input and output issues are quite common in colleges, but much less so than they are in PreK–12 programs. As a professor, you may have a student with a learning disability once or a handful of times each academic year. College students who have no disabilities, but who do have different learning styles, generally have made whatever adjustments they are going to make. (Those who made ineffective adjustments usually did not make it to this level of education.) As a college or university professor, you should expect that the student knows what to do and how to do it: you should expect the same level of academic performance from this student as you do from other students. Academic freedom allows you considerable leeway in how much, if any, changes you will accept (e.g., allowing a student to write a paper in lieu of taking a test).

UNIVERSAL DESIGN IN CONTINUING AND ADULT EDUCATION

Continuing and adult education is subject to the same disability laws as are colleges and universities. That is, the standard is one of "nondiscrimination" on behalf of students with disabilities and students from minority groups. The major differences are: (1) Academic performance is not measured and (2) institutional pressure upon you as a teacher is much more to make the course enjoyable, and thus profitable, than it is to uphold academic standards.

As in colleges and universities, the student is required to bring any special needs or preferences to the attention of a program official. If the continuing/adult education program is sponsored by a college, this will often be the college's special services coordinator. If it is sponsored by a local or county government, this may be the "ADA compliance officer" (who may have a different, but similar, title). This person acts at the student's request. Your obligation as teacher is to permit whatever accommodations that person arranges.

Sensory and mobility limitations are much more common at this level than they are in PreK–12 schools or in colleges. You will most frequently see hearing impairments that are well short of deafness (the student has some difficulty understanding what you say, and often asks you to repeat things), visual impairments that require special glasses or magnifying devices but do not call for Braille or taped texts, and mobility impairments that slow down but do not prevent ambulation.

THE SEVEN PRINCIPLES IN EDUCATION

In Chapter 2, the principles were introduced. Here, they are applied to education. Subsequent chapters will offer much greater elaboration upon how each may assist educators.

Principle One: Equitable Use

<u>Definition</u>: The design is useful and marketable to people with diverse abilities.

This is probably the cardinal principle behind the idea of universal design: make accessibility appealing to the vast majority of users, in this case, prospective and actual students.

Guideline 1a: Provide the same means of use for all users: identical whenever possible; equivalent when not.

This guideline instructs us to do what universal design generally tells us: try to make general education, in all its richness, available to students with different needs. You should resort to substitutions only where necessary. See the next guideline for one reason why.

Guideline 1b: Avoid segregating or stigmatizing any users.

"Separate but equal" is rarely equal. The U.S. Supreme Court told us that in the landmark 1954 decision in *Brown v. Board of Education*. Segregating students is not usually as intentional as it was in that case. Unintentional or not, separation can lead to stigmatization. As a teacher, you should find ways to integrate education wherever possible. One of many examples: pre-screen Internet resources you recommend to students, making sure that those resources are accessible (see Chapter 8). A good example is the Web site for "PlanetMath" (*www.planemath.com*). Created with help from scientists at the National Aeronautics and Space Administration (NASA), this site teaches mathematical concepts by asking students to consider problems they might encounter in dealing with airplanes. It was designed so that users immediately encounter a text version of the material (the accessible version) and only upon selecting the graphics-rich alternative would they see an inaccessible version. See also "Chemtutor" (*www.chemtutor.com*), which offers high school and college level chemistry material. Chemtutor has some graphics, but overall it is a text-friendly site. Both serve the needs of general and special students alike, without any unnecessary stigmatization. Students who have special needs visit the same sites and find there the same information as do students with no special needs.

That is the basic idea. Another illustration: when I have students with learning disabilities in one of my courses, I announce in class that disks containing my lectures (as prepared for delivery) are available upon request. People with dyslexia and other learning disabilities often do much better when they listen to materials than when they read it (see Chapter 4). By giving them a disk, I provide them with text that they can listen to with a speech synthesizer. What I do not do is to tell only students I know to have dyslexia about these disks. That would segregate them and, (once others in the class found out, as they inevitably would) stigmatize them as well. I also allow students, not just those with learning disabilities or visual impairments, to tape record my lectures.

Guideline 1c: Make provisions for privacy, security, and safety equally available to all users.

In education, safety issues arise primarily during night hours, when students leave classroom buildings for dorms or for cars. Good exterior lighting, adequate campus security staff, and related steps help. Another example: The 1990s have witnessed widespread abuse of "handicapped parking" spaces. An incredible number of students, at Hofstra and elsewhere, demonstrate no compunction at all about usurping handicapped parking spaces. They justify their abuse by saying that they are busy, their time is limited, parking is scarce; more often, though, their actual motivation seems to be to get "the best spot." I have seen a 22-year-old woman pull into a handicapped parking space, fully 20 minutes before class began, just to sit in the car, happy to have secured such a desirable parking space. Only much later, when her car had been towed and she had to pay a $130 fine, was she apologetic about using her grandfather's special parking permit.

Guideline 1d: Make the design appealing to all users.

This is particularly important with respect to students from minority cultures and for older learners. As Chapter 1 suggested, there are simple steps you can take, such as screening course materials to eliminate unnecessary references to "individual" achievement at the expense of family values. Some cultures stress group and family goals, as opposed to the individual accomplishments that are highlighted in northern European cultures. As another example: many older people prefer to take courses in the morning hours, as opposed to afternoon or evening hours. There is recent research showing that they tend to perform better in the morning, too (Intons-Peterson, et al., 1999). The clear implication: if your desire is to appeal to seniors, schedule your course for early in the day, if at all feasible.

Principle Two: Flexibility in Use

Definition: The design accommodates a wide range of individual preferences and abilities.

This principle teaches us to try to meet individual needs, rather than to aim for the "middle" and hope that people on both sides will somehow adjust. The idea applies directly to education as well as to architecture, interior design, product design, and other fields of human factors.

Guideline 2a: Provide choices in methods of use.

Some students prefer participating in a group activity over producing a personal term paper, while some would rather perform community service than take a test. If the alternatives serve learning in your course, you should let them.

Guideline 2b: Accommodate right- or left-handed access and use.

This is not a big problem in education, aside from the need for left-handed desks—for some reason I can't fathom, under 10% of desks in the classrooms I've used are for left-handers. Aside from scavenging for additional desks, there is not much to be done in education to follow this guideline.

Guideline 2c: Facilitate the user's accuracy and precision.

Remember from personal experience which ideas, words, etc., are especially difficult for students to learn and present these concepts with ample illustrations and elaboration. Every field of study has its own lexicon, or vocabulary, and uses words in particular ways. A good teacher never forgets which ones were, at first, hard to understand and/or remember, and places special emphasis on these in the classroom.

Guideline 2d: Provide adaptability to the user's pace.

This is best done using PCs (see Chapter 4) and the Web (see Chapter 8) because with these, people can read and write at their own speed. Regardless of whether or not you use technology in your instruction, the key is to give students the time they need. I have found it helpful, after enunciating a key idea, to pause briefly. Such pauses help even my fastest students, because they have an opportunity to think about what they've just heard. I also give examples. These illustrations allow the faster students to see different aspects of central ideas; they have the added benefit, for learning disabled students, of providing the time that is needed to understand what has already been said. With respect to reading materials, I have found it much more helpful to require a limited amount of reading, rather than too much; carefully selected materials offer the essential information and obviate the need for students to do additional reading. Of course, I use the same guidelines in my own writing: I write as much as is needed to explain something clearly, and then I stop. I find it useful to bear in mind the so-called 80/20 rule—80% of what is worth knowing is contained in 20% of what you assign (even your own writing).

Principle Three: Simple and Intuitive Use

Definition: Use of the design is easy to understand, regardless of the user's experience, knowledge, language skills, or current concentration level.

Hardware and software programs developed during the late 1970s and early 1980s were characterized by a distressing unusability. Computer scientists, engineers, and programmers created products that pleased them—seemingly oblivious to the fact that most people do not think like they do. Today, we know better: the ultimate test of a product is not whether computer types find it cool but whether end users can understand it and benefit from it. This principle is also directly applicable when you have students with attention deficits in your class—their concentration level (at least with respect to what you are trying to teach them) may vary considerably during any given class period.

Guideline 3a: Eliminate unnecessary complexity.

This is a basic principle of education. As a professor, my interest is in helping my students to master certain data and particular ideas. When I choose a textbook for the course, I look for one that provides this information in an "accessible" way (meaning, in this instance, readily understood by my students). Students in my course on physical disabilities routinely tell me that they really like my text, *Physical, Sensory, and Health Disabilities* (Prentice Hall / Merrill Education, 2000) because it "reads so easily" and because it is "so brief" as compared to competing texts. I am not insulted by such comments. To the contrary, doing those things were goals I had in writing the book.

In teaching undergraduate students, I assign reading that I know they can understand. Learning a new subject is difficult enough. It is my job to clear the way so that my students can do that, unimpeded. As long as a source provides the necessary information, a readily usable one is preferable to a dense, hard-to-read alternative. No purpose is served by insisting that they read the same primary sources, including peer-reviewed journal articles, that I do. That would add a layer of complexity to their education without enriching their learning. With graduate students, however, I do insist that they read professional journal articles. I do that because I believe that the ability to read such materials is one they will need throughout their careers.

The same idea serves me when I design or update my Web page; because people having a wide range of knowledge and skills visit that page, I deliberately chose plain, unadorned backgrounds and dark, sharply defined letters and characters, as these provide maximum contrast, thus improving readability. Were I to succumb to the inducements of multi-colored and complex backgrounds, I would unnecessarily impede my visitors' progress.

Guideline 3b: Be consistent with user expectations and intuition.

In education, the most obvious application of this guideline is: Describe the course accurately. Prospective students have a right to know, before they sign up, exactly what will, and will not, be taught in a particular course. I follow the same principle in testing: I give my students a "study guide" two or three weeks in advance of a major test. I write that study guide after I prepare the test, so that I can be certain that the guide accurately describes the test—and that nothing on the test will really surprise the students. Information kiosks on the campus should also do what students think they do, in ways students anticipate they will: use should be intuitive, even for first-time users.

Guideline 3c: Accommodate a wide range of literacy and language skills.

There are, of course, limitations in how completely teachers can follow this guideline. If students lack mastery of any language, they are not prepared to take college-level or graduate courses, and there is basically nothing a teacher can do to change that. I have taught students who understood my lectures (in English) but who were very limited in their ability to demonstrate their knowledge—these students were much better in receptive than in expressive use of the language. As a professor, I need to take into account the cognitive load these students bore as they mentally translated what they wanted to say, from Spanish into English, and then struggled to answer essay questions in their second language. Most of these students turned in term papers that were difficult for me to read. I found it useful to question these students, one-on-one, orally, so as to understand what they did, and did not, know about the subject matter; even better would have been to bring a translator to those one-on-one sessions. I approach these issues in a certain way, being a professor in a graduate school. My attitude is that my job is to teach the content that these students need in order to succeed in a profession. Knowing that writing clear English is important in their chosen professions, I refer them to bilingual tutoring services and urge them to take advantage of those. Elementary school teachers may well hold different expectations and thus will require different things from their students.

Today, if a student is fluent in, say, Spanish or French, but not in English, there are steps teachers can take to assist those students. Chapter 5 introduces computer-based language translation software that is getting better with each passing year. Realistically, in 2000, it is not yet good enough: a fluent speaker of the target language is still required to polish the result. Still, that is a relatively small step. Just a few years ago, a translator was needed to transpose the entire document. Given the nationwide shortage of skilled translators, that was both a time-consuming and an expensive proposition (they charge 35 cents per word, on average; to appreciate that number, consider that translating this relatively short book into Portuguese or German could easily set you back $17,500). By contrast, the investment of less than $100 for the software, plus perhaps another $200 to the translator for polishing up the manuscript, should suffice to produce Spanish, French, etc., versions of articles and book chapters. See *www.lhsl.com* for more information about language translation software.

Guideline 3d: Arrange information consistent with its importance.

This is another cardinal idea of education. My time in the classroom with my students is severely limited; we meet for less than two hours each week for 15 weeks. Given those constraints, I can only lecture about selected topics. I have to choose the most important of them. My doing so gives the students an "organizer" or scaffolding that helps them as they read the textbook to recognize which ideas are the most important.

Guideline 3e: Provide effective prompting and feedback during and after task completion.

Concrete feedback is especially appreciated by students who have learning disabilities. They often benefit, too, from instructor-provided "scaffolding," or advance organizers, which assist them in understanding how different concepts relate to each other. Actually, advance scaffolding helps any student to follow a lecture and to organize lecture notes.

Principle Four: Perceptible Information

Definition: The design communicates necessary information effectively to the user, regardless of ambient conditions or the user's sensory abilities.

This is one of Ron Mace's real contributions to universal design. He understood that people with no disabilities sometimes faced the kinds of problems that people with disabilities constantly confronted. By insisting that universal design accommodate the temporary needs of non-disabled persons, Ron broadened the idea's appeal.

Guideline 4a: Use different modes (pictorial, verbal, tactile) for redundant presentation of essential information.

Redundancy is one of the crucial elements of access (Bowe, 1984). Receptive communication (what is said or otherwise presented to the student), if offered auditorially, should also be available visually. By the same token, expressive communication (what communication the student presents), if available visually, should also be accepted auditorially. Rochester Institute of Technology supports a Web site known as "EASI" (Equal Access to Software Information) at *www.rit.edu/~easi/*. This site provides help on making educational materials accessible. (It also offers details on distance-learning courses the EASI project sponsors.)

Guideline 4b: Maximize "legibility" of essential information.

The World Wide Web is, in effect, a huge library of "books" with no pages to turn. Insofar as the "pages" in Web sites are accessible—today, a tenuous assumption but something that is becoming more and more commonplace—the information one may find on the Web is a terrific way to extend the boundaries of knowledge for students and working adults alike. The key to making Web pages accessible is "text" (unadorned words). Text is the graphics-free format that LYNX, a browser widely used by people who are blind or have dyslexia, presents. Popular browsers, such as Netscape's Navigator™, offer up both graphics and text, and thus are less accessible. (Details: Chapter 8.)

Guideline 4c: Differentiate elements in ways that can be described (i.e., make it easy to give instructions or directions).

The original intent of this guideline was to ensure that people who are blind or have low vision would receive spoken instructions or directions that clearly and simply told them what they needed to know. As such, the guideline most obviously applies to maps. In the classroom, it also relates to directions. A sighted student telling a blind student where the chalk is would be well-advised to use the clock metaphor ("The chalk is at your 3 o'clock"). One explaining how far away the door is should also adopt a universal measure: "It's about 20 feet straight ahead of you." This guideline warns people not to say things like "It's approximately 15 steps ahead," because the strides of different people vary.

Guideline 4d: Provide compatibility with a variety of techniques or devices used by people with sensory limitations.

At least some of the telephones in dorms and in classroom buildings should be hearing-aid compatible. Kiosks and other machines from which students retrieve important information (such as grades!) should have "active" rather than "passive" displays (active displays are compatible with some assistive devices, such as the Optacon™ while passive displays are not). The small camera of the Optacon™ needs images it can "read" in order to translate them into tactile versions that people who are blind can read.

Principle Five: Tolerance for Error

Definition: The design minimizes hazards and the adverse consequences of accidental or unintended actions.

This idea is much more relevant for devices than for education, but the concept can help us. If we can prevent students from making mistakes that we can foresee, but they may not, that will help them to learn better.

Guideline 5a: Arrange elements to minimize hazards and errors: most used elements, most accessible; hazardous elements eliminated, isolated, or shielded.

The kiosks at Hofstra are designed to allow students to "recover" from an error without consequence; they can exit from the sections on grades if they incorrectly enter an identification number, for example. I put a "home" hotlink on each "page" of my Web site so that if visitors decide they took a "wrong turn" they can quickly and painlessly recover. To illustrate the guideline with PC applications, consider SlowKeys and BounceKeys (both built into Windows^{tm}— Control Panel"). SlowKeys causes the computer to recognize, and implement, a keystroke only if a deliberate, rather strong depression is made; SlowKeys ignores glancing hits on keys, assuming them to be unintended, accidental key strokes—which, for many people with cerebral palsy as well as some with quadriplegia or stroke, are exactly what they are! BounceKeys helps people who have tremors, including some who had strokes and some with Parkinson's disease. The program will not accept the same key hit twice in rapid succession. If you touch the same key twice, but with your usual time interval in between, BounceKeys accepts your input.

Guideline 5b: Provide warnings of hazards and errors.

If attendance at your lectures is essential for passing the course, as it is with mine, you should find a way to alert students of this in advance. At Hofstra, word of mouth usually suffices: my students know when they enroll in one of my courses that I am one of the professors whose classes they cannot safely miss. In my first few years here, however, I had to "suggest" to students that they make an extra effort to be present at each class meeting.

Guideline 5c: Provide fail safe features.

Some professors allow students to re-write papers after those have been marked up. If I were teaching English, I would do so. After all, in writing this manuscript, I have been able to make numerous revisions without penalty. Another example: I save work like this on my hard drive at home, on a floppy that I take between home and Hofstra, and on my hard drive at Hofstra. This may be overkill, but my sense of it is that when I spend a year to two years researching and writing a manuscript, saving the work in three places is not an excessive precaution.

Guideline 5d: Discourage unconscious action in tasks that require vigilance.

I ask someone else to proofread my writing before I submit it to a journal or a book publisher. I have learned from experience that my eyes "see," not what I have actually written, but rather what I intended to write. For this reason, I cannot effectively proofread my own work. Finding and correcting errors is so important that it requires the little extra effort that is involved in third-party proofreading. My students at Hofstra rarely ask anyone to proofread their term papers before they submit them to me; I keep asking them to do so, and keep being disappointed. Semester after semester, I keep being reminded that the human mind is simply not designed for proofreading its own creations.

Principle Six: Low Physical Effort
<u>Definition</u>: The design can be used efficiently and comfortably and with a minimum of fatigue.

The obvious correlate of this principle to teaching is distance learning (see Chapter 6). However, if you interpret the term "low physical effort" broadly, there are other implications in this principle for educators.

Guideline 6a: Allow user to maintain a neutral body position.

Students using wheelchairs should be able to position the chair under a writing surface and there write or type without straining shoulders, arms, wrists, or fingers. Generally, this means that the writing surface should be adjustable where possible. If fixed, it should be about 27 inches from the floor (allowing room for the knees and the footrest) and no more than about 19 inches deep (from the outer edge to the controls or keys the student is expected to reach).

Guideline 6b: Use reasonable operating forces.

What is "reasonable" will depend on the student. With young children, door-opening pressures should be much lower than is acceptable in facilities used primarily by adults. At colleges and universities, the pressure levels should be selected on the basis of what meets the needs of 5–foot, 100–pound adults, not those of 6–foot, 200–pound security officers.

Guideline 6c: Minimize repetitive actions.

Computer software variously known as "word expansion" or "word prediction" programs are an excellent example. These programs quickly learn the user's preferred vocabulary and can complete a word or phrase once the first few letters have been typed. Over the course of a ten-page term paper, such programs can save as much as half an hour of typing. They are well worth their modest costs.

Guideline 6d: Minimize sustained physical effort.

Many of my students work full-time during the day before coming to my classes in the evening. It is a lot to ask them to sit nearly motionless for two hours. The time seems to go by much faster if I give them occasional opportunities to do different things, i.e., meet in small groups for discussion, accompany me on a brief trip across campus, and the like.

Principle Seven: Size and Space for Approach and Use
<u>Definition</u>: Appropriate size and space is provided for approach, reach, manipulation, and use regardless of user's body size, posture, or mobility.
    As suggested above (see 6a), the height, depth, etc., of desks and other writing surfaces matter. Chapter 7 offers brief highlights of some of the most important reach dimensions.

Guideline 7a: Provide a clear line of sight to important elements for any seated or standing user.

The most obvious, and perhaps most violated, example: try to avoid "talking to the blackboard." More students than you realize need to see your face and lips in order to understand your speech.

Guideline 7b: Make reach to all components comfortable for any seated or standing user.

This matters most in rest rooms, in kiosk areas, and in classrooms or labs where students use PCs. The minimum and maximum reach lengths discussed in Chapter 7 help with these.

Guideline 7c: Accommodate variations in hand and grip size.

Door levers are excellent examples of following this guideline. A student in one of my classes stands just three feet, three inches tall. He has very small hands. He told me he's just delighted with door levers because they are so easy for him to use. Door knobs, by contrast, are all but impossible for him: they require people to reach the knob easily (many are too high for him to do this readily), grasp the knob firmly (he can't), and twist sharply (hard for him).

Guideline 7d: Provide adequate space for the use of assistive devices or personal assistance.

This guideline is an obvious factor arguing in favor of moveable as opposed to fixed student desks and chairs. Only if desks/chairs are moveable can scooters, wheelchairs, crutches, and the like easily be stored next to the student's desk, yet not obstruct the movement of other students.

Chapter 4

Principles One and Two

PRINCIPLE ONE: EQUITABLE USE

<u>Definition</u>: The design is useful and marketable to people with diverse abilities.

Universal design will only be accepted by non-disabled persons if it somehow meets their needs as well as those of people with disabilities. Accordingly, providing the same services to disabled and non-disabled users, insofar as this is possible, is important. An added benefit of this approach is that people with special needs are not segregated or placed apart from people with no special needs.

Guideline 1a: Provide the same means of use for all users: identical whenever possible; equivalent when not.

In general, educators should teach nontraditional students in the same ways they teach traditional students, unless one or more of the nontraditional students requests something different. This is not to say that teachers should not alter the ways in which they teach all students. They should. I have found it useful, for example, to prepare all of my lectures on disk and to copy that disk (if no student requests it, at least I have a back-up of work that consumed several hours of my time). I tell all my students that this information is available to them: I have no way of knowing which, or how many, students who do not have disabilities nonetheless prefer to listen to, rather than or in addition to reading, materials.

I also tell them that much of what they need to research, and read, is available either on my Web site or on other sites that are hot-linked to my Web page. The point is that I make these things available to the traditional as well as the nontraditional students, in a nondiscriminatory way. When I cannot provide the same information in the same ways to all my students, I try to ensure that what they get is truly equivalent to what other students get. As an example: I try to refer students only to accessible Web sites (details: Chapter 8). As another example: I try to avoid discussing important ideas orally in class if I have not also made the same information available on disk or in some other appropriate medium. Note the repeated use of "I try": it is not always possible to do these things.

Distance learning is another way of implementing this guideline (see Chapter 6). Done properly, it offers very similar services to students, although it is not, of course, identical to in-person instruction.

Guideline 1b: Avoid segregating or stigmatizing any users.

When I tell my classes that information is available on disk or in other alternative formats, I tell all of them this. My experience has been that within a week or so, a student or two will e-mail me to request material in other media, not because he, she, or they have learning disabilities, but because of a personal preference for learning in different ways. That is why this guideline is useful: by following it, teachers avoid stigmatizing students with learning disabilities, because nondisabled students are also using these other media.

Guideline 1c: Make provisions for privacy, security, and safety.

Distance learning is an alternative that appeals to students worried about their safety away from home, especially at night. It is important for teachers to permit voice telephony, as opposed to video telephony, if requested by a student. Members of some cultures may regard video telephony as unacceptably invasive of the family's privacy. The principle extends much further than this, of course. When students who need extra time take exams in different locations, their privacy and security must be assured. Other students, and of course non-students, should never be told where and when the alternative test is being administered.

If you have students read each others' work, for whatever reason (this can be helpful in English composition classes, for example), the papers should be identified by Social Security Number or campus I.D. number or some other indicator that preserves personal privacy. For the same reason, when I return tests or papers after grading them, I always "hide" the grade on an inside sheet, so fellow students cannot observe the scores.

Guideline 1d: Make the design appealing to all users.

Some cultures promote interpersonal cooperation rather than, or over, interpersonal competition. For people from such cultures, opportunities to learn together make courses appealing. They may appreciate the option of working as a team on a project, or spending class time in small-group discussion, or both, more than will some students from traditional cultures.

The classroom itself can also be made more appealing by use of moveable rather than fixed chairs. Several factors argue for chairs that may be moved. One has already been mentioned: it makes group work much easier. Another is cultural: some people like to be close to friends, while others like more "breathing room." A third is practical: movement of people who use wheelchairs, walkers, and other devices is facilitated when chairs can be moved away from a path of travel. A final example has to do with assistance animals: guide dogs need room to lie down in places where they will not be in the path of people trying to walk past them.

PRINCIPLE TWO: FLEXIBILITY IN USE

Definition: The design accommodates a wide range of individual preferences and abilities.

This is a key principle in education. Different students learn in different ways, at different paces, and universally designed education must respond to those divergences.

Guideline 2a: Provide choice in methods of use.

Fortunately, educators have available to them a wide array of options. So, too, do students. If your students need, or prefer, to do some things differently, you should permit this as long as it does not detract from the learning experience.

Cultural Choices

Two needs for such choices were discussed briefly in Chapter 1: the desire of many families, especially families from minority cultures, to avoid invasion of the family's privacy and the need to reduce stress upon other family members. Providing flexibility in course scheduling is a method of responding to the fact that traditional schedules sometimes place additional stress upon other family members, who must perform extra work so that the student may attend class.

Another illustration draws from my experience on Long Island. In recent years, large numbers of immigrants have settled on the island. We had a student from India recently who was concerned about following Muslim tradition, which teaches, among other things, that she should avoid physical contact with others. That can be a problem in college. As an example: during the graduation ceremony, deans and the college president routinely shake hands with the new graduates as they hand them their diplomas. As it happens, she came up with an innovative solution (she accepted the diploma by grasping it in her right hand, thus making shaking hands a problem for the dean, and, just to be sure, kept her left hand firmly at her side). That worked. Better, perhaps, would have been a quiet conversation with the dean in advance of the ceremony, expressing her preferences and requesting cooperation. That might have been less awkward for all concerned.

The PC

Personal computers offer tremendous opportunities for teachers and students alike to customize the ways in which information is presented and the ways in which students interact with it. Students may change the size of text, making it smaller or larger. They may alter the fonts used, choosing those they find easiest to read. They may adjust the colors used—both the background color(s) and the foreground/text colors. Or they may listen to the text, either instead of reading it or while reading it. Students may answer chapter-ending questions by highlighting and pasting selected sentences or even paragraphs, perhaps then editing that text, or they may compose their own answers anew.

The traditional textbook, by contrast, can only be used in a very limited number of ways. Material is presented in one sequence; students generally must read it in the same order, although they may, by making liberal use of indexes, read in a sequence they themselves select. Chapter-ending questions can only be answered in two basic ways: one, by memory, and two, by paging back to re-read selected text.

An interesting use of computers to present material in a customized way was illustrated by Aronson and Colet (1997). They compared "Rapid Serial Visual Presentation" (RSVP) to traditional straight text. (A distressing number of people in the late 1990s adopted the acronym "RSVP" for their creations. Soon after reading Aronson and Colet, I attended an advisory group meeting in which a program for the Social Security Administration was introduced; it, too, was called "RSVP." Neither that program, nor the rapid-reading one, has anything to do with courtesy in responding to invitations.) In Aronson and Colet's program, each succeeding word overwrites the preceding word; as the name suggests, the words are offered serially. This is not a new idea; it dates back to the 1960s. What is new, however, is evidence demonstrating that RSVP significantly increases speed of reading for many students, without compromising understanding. Importantly, it allowed readers to control the rate at which the words appeared on-screen. Robert Bailey (1999) later showed that with RSVP people can read as much as three times faster than they can in traditional ways. It is possible, although neither Aronson and Colet (1997) nor Bailey (1999) demonstrated it, that RSVP may help some students who have certain kinds of learning disabilities, in part because RSVP virtually eliminates eye movements (saccades) and in part because it offers each word by itself, with no distractions. It would be interesting to see if students with dyslexia and some other reading disorders do better with serially presented words than with words strung together one after another.

Listservs

Some students learn best by having opportunities to interact with other students. Such discussion between students can be time consuming, but not if the teacher provides opportunities for virtually unlimited discussion by creating a listserv. In education, the listserv can also be called an "electronic study circle," wrote Pamela Kleiber, Margaret Holt, and Jill Swenson (1998), who provided a detailed description of the method in "The Electronic Forum": (*www.cpn.org/sections/tools/manuals/electronic_handbook1.html*).

A listserv, for those who have not yet experienced this technology, is simply a linked list of e-mail addresses. Each student in the class gives the instructor his or her e-mail address. The teacher then compiles those addresses into a list. The name and e-mail address of the list is given to each student. From that point on, the instructor can e-mail every student in the class, simultaneously, simply by addressing e-mail to the listserv name. The students may do likewise. Within seconds (or minutes, depending on Internet traffic volume) each student receives a copy of any message posted by the teacher or by any other student.

Very importantly, listservs take advantage of the fact that students who have special needs or learning styles already have configured their home PCs to meet their desires. Thus, students who learn best by listening can turn on a speech synthesizer and hear all messages; a student who needs large print can read the messages in 24-point or even larger type. Similarly, a student whose learning disability makes it difficult for her to navigate in graphics-rich environments can set up the e-mail facility to display simple text (and only text). Notice that, in compliance with Guideline 1c, other students are not aware of their classmates' at-home adaptations.

Kleiber, Holt, and Swenson (1998) pointed out that a great "plus" of listservs in education is that this discussion takes place outside of class meeting times. This means that student interaction can continue as long as any of the students wishes, without cutting into the time available for in-person instruction. Another big advantage is that the instructor can instantly alert all students to any change in schedule or assignments, simply by posting an e-mail message to the listserv (this can prove to be very helpful during inclement weather, or if the instructor is called away on an emergency). The same capability proves to be very useful when an article is published that directly relates to what the students are reading, or an event connected to the course's content occurs: the instructor can instantly tell the entire class about it, rather than having to wait until the next class meeting.

There are other advantages. Any in-person class tends to be dominated, to one extent or another, by students who are verbally fluent and who like to lead discussions. E-mail-based listservs are much less susceptible to such manipulation. Any student who tires of another's endless postings can simply, quickly, and easily delete that person's messages (without even reading them, if the student so desires). Students log on to the listserv when it is convenient for them, and log off when they wish. And messages may be, and often are, anonymous. This has the advantage of presenting ideas on their own, as pure ideas, and thus allows for those ideas to be evaluated on their own (as opposed to in-person comments).

Disadvantages to listservs are similar to those of e-mail. We cannot see other participants, so we do not benefit from reading their "body language" or other nonverbal messages; this can make realizing that someone is joking problematic. (To prevent misunderstandings, the teacher can forbid sarcasm and can ask students to attach smiley faces to messages whenever they are joking.)

As a variation on listservs, I have my students exchange e-mail addresses. This takes perhaps five to ten minutes. It enables the students to connect with each other, at their convenience, e.g., to network. Thus, two students with identical or similar term-paper topics can share ideas with each other. Similarly, two or more students may "study together" without leaving their homes.

Guideline 2b: Accommodate right- or left-handed access and use.

About 10% of Americans are left-handed and another 3% are ambidextrous. Designers and engineers, following the age-old "90% principle" have usually developed for right-handers; this includes not only people who design and make student desks for classrooms but also computer keyboards (notice that virtually all numeric pads are on the right side) and other devices and facilities used in education. There is a powerful cultural preference in many countries for right-handedness, such that just 1% of Japanese adults write using their left hands. That this is a cultural and not a genetic bias is demonstrated by the fact that 5% of Japanese boys and 3% of girls in first grade wrote using their left hands, but just 0.2% of boys and no girls did so by 8th grade (Corballis, 1997).

Much more confusing, and thus less helpful for educators, is research on handedness in hearing. A recent study illustrates: Reib and Reib (1998) tested right-handed individuals. They found that most heard better using their left ears—that is, they had less hearing loss in those ears than in their right ears. Despite this fact, they tended to perform better when listening with their right ears. Asked if they had a preference, most said they did, for the right ear. I interpret these findings as relating to relatively mild levels of hearing loss, and, equally important, to people's ability to learn. When hearing level is within normal ranges, most individuals can adjust, unconsciously, for slight impairments in one as opposed to the other ear. I do not believe the research is conclusive enough to inform teachers about where to stand when lecturing. Perhaps future studies will shed some light on this question.

Several years ago, I encountered an unexpected variation on handedness. A student of mine was a "mirror writer": she wrote on a translucent sheet, which she then reversed and handed to me when the exam was over. My job was to accept this unusual method of test-taking; at 42 years of age, she was not interested in learning a new way of writing. (As a professor in a graduate school, I took the attitude that my job was to accept her writing as I found it and to facilitate her learning what she needed to know; in this, and in some other ways, my job differs from that of an elementary school teacher.) Later, when she applied to begin her student teaching, the field placement staff at the university were concerned. When they consulted me, I explained that every school has overhead projectors in classrooms: all this woman had to do was to flip an overhead transparency, and her students would see perfectly composed, "ordinary" left-to-right handwriting. (This woman obviously did not use blackboards in her teaching.)

Guideline 2c: Facilitate the user's accuracy and precision.

Screen Size

If your students work with computer monitors, they will probably perform better with 19-inch monitors. Studies conducted by Compaq Computer Corporation[R] (Simmons & Manahan, 1999) and by researchers at the University of Maryland (DiPierro, Nachman, & Raderman, 2000) suggest that people do better, in less time, when using 19-inch monitors as compared to 15-inch, 17-inch, and even 21-inch monitors. This holds true for detail work such as word processing and also for surfing on the Web.

Speech Recognition

Some students cannot type accurately. This includes many who have such physical disabilities as cerebral palsy, as well as some who have learning disabilities. Computer speech recognition can help in both cases—but different kinds of voice recognition software are required. Most people who have cerebral palsy do not pronounce words consistently enough to allow them to use such popular and inexpensive "continuous" speech recognition programs as Dragon Systems' Naturally Speaking[tm] (details: *www.dragon.com*). Instead, they need what is called a "discrete" speech recognition program. Dragon offers one: Dragon Dictate[tm]. Lernout & Hauspie, the Belgian company that owns Dragon Dictate[tm], has one: Kurzweil Voicepad[tm] (details: *www.lhsl.com*). These discrete programs require speakers to pause after each word. They also require more pre-use training of the software. Often, they require users to adopt the military alphabet ("Alpha," "Beta," "Charlie," et cetera) for spelling out words. The flip side is that these are more robust programs, more capable of handling "different" speech, including that of people with cerebral palsy, people who have been deaf since birth, or people who have had a stroke. Continuous speech recognition programs such as Dragon Naturally Speaking[tm] do not respond well to such "different" voices, because the programs require users to say words very much the same way each time.

All of us should approach computer speech recognition with a healthy dose of skepticism, now and for the next several years. Although advertisements claim that continuous speech recognition programs such as Naturally Speaking[tm] can bring "conversational speed" to the task, in reality people do not much exceed 30 to 40 words per minute. That is because the software often is not sure what the spoken word actually was (it responds with a pull-down menu of possibilities rather than with a definite "hit," requiring the user to add, "Select 4," to indicate that the fourth, rather than the first, item on the menu is the desired one). It is also because the program often "guesses" wrong. Even at 95% accuracy, which seems to be high, one out of every 20 words is incorrect. With a typical page of text comprising some 500 words, this means error-correction of 25 words. That takes quite a bit of time.

Speech Synthesis

It is not only input that is difficult for some students. Some, including people who have dyslexia, a common learning disability, have problems reading. Lernout & Hauspie introduced in early January, 2000, a program called L&H Kurzweil 3000[tm]. This program assists people with learning and reading disabilities to increase their speed and accuracy of reading. Included is L&H RealSpeak[tm], a speech synthesis program (it talks). Important for educators: L&H Kurzweil 3000[tm] also features a test-taking module. This lets teachers scan in tests, which then appear on a PC screen. As students take the test, they listen to it (using RealSpeak[tm]) and then enter answers by clicking the mouse pointer at the appropriate place and typing their answers. The module speaks the letters, words, and sentences that the student types, allowing the student to proofread his or her answers. (Details: *www.lhsl.com*).

Guideline 2d: Provide adaptability to the user's pace.
When a teacher lectures, students with some kinds of learning disabilities frequently become unsure of what they have heard: "Did he say 'bat'? Or was it 'pat'? Or maybe 'mat'?" They have to, in effect, stop listening to the lecture while they figure this out. Thus, the next sentence, or several sentences, that the teacher says will not be listened to by these students. For this reason, students who have attention deficit disorders (ADD) or attention deficit hyperactivity disorder (ADHD) are at times unavailable for learning. Knowing that one or more students have learning disabilities or attention deficits, educators should slow down, notably by giving examples or more simply by repeating important messages. In this way, teachers give students with learning disabilities the time they need to process previously spoken sentences and give students with ADD/ADHD more opportunities to attend.

When sign language interpreters are used in the classroom to translate for deaf students, the pace of instruction usually is not affected. However, some interpreters are not skilled enough to keep up with such a pace. If the interpreter being used in the classroom is not a fully certified individual, the instructor may need to slow down the lecture. With respect to students who have low vision, a good rule to remember is that it takes much longer to read a given amount of text when that material is enlarged (magnified); when students are expected to read in classrooms, teachers should allow extra time for students with vision losses. (Details: *www.rid.org.*)

Students from some cultural minority backgrounds, particularly Hispanic and Native American families, will tend not to speak up in class. Their cultures teach them that this is a sign of respect for their teachers. Other students, not from those backgrounds, simply are shy. I have found that it sometimes takes half the semester for me to "warm up" these students so that they participate in class. It is important that I allow them this time, rather than expect them to speak up during the first several meetings of the class. However, because I believe that class participation is important for all my students, and because I am not a person who believes that continuous student silence is a sign of respect for me, I try to engage them at about mid-term. When I do, I make a concerted effort to praise them for speaking up, to find something positive and noteworthy about what they say, and to bring the attention of other students to those comments. This generally has the effect of reinforcing the long-delayed participation.

Some cultures make a point of valuing people's contributions to the family over their individual achievements. If you have students who hold such beliefs in one of your classes, and they request an extension of time to complete an academic project due to family needs, you should grant their request unless doing so would seriously compromise their education. I struggled with this issue early in my career, because my own cultural values told me to complete my work on time, even if I had to work very long hours to do so and still do things my family expected. I now realize that this was my culture guiding me. It is not an absolute. Accordingly, I am now much more amenable to granting requests so that my students may do things they regard as important.

Chapter 5

Principles Three and Four

PRINCIPLE THREE: SIMPLE AND INTUITIVE USE

Definition: Use of the design is easy to understand, regardless of the user's experience, knowledge, language skills, or current concentration level.

This is a very important principle in education. Whether we are talking about the textbooks we select for student use in a course, or the lectures we present, or the activities we plan for classes, a prime consideration should be that these are understandable to, and easily used by, our students.

Guideline 3a: Eliminate unnecessary complexity.

Teachers well know that every discipline has its own jargon and its own way of "thinking." These words, and these "logical" thought processes, are not, however, intuitive to students encountering the discipline for the first time. To illustrate, when I teach a graduate course on special education law, one of the definitions in the law is that for "specific learning disability." I know that many of my students—being unfamiliar with special education and not knowing yet what all the different disabilities are—will interpret this term to be a term referring to all disabilities. That is, they may think that any disability that affects education is, *ipso facto*, a "learning disability." Being aware of this, I tell them right away that this term in fact refers only to one particular kind of disability. Williams (1998), reviewing the literature on multimedia in education, added this important point: New information should be presented more slowly. As teachers, we know (or should know) what ideas and terms are unfamiliar to our students; Williams urged us to make a conscious effort to introduce that material in a deliberate fashion. By doing these things, we prevent students from making mistakes; we are, that is, eliminating unnecessary complexity.

Guideline 3b: Be consistent with user expectations and intuition.

As a teacher, I need to be predictable in how I use class time. My students quickly learn that I lecture only about key ideas in their textbooks; they know that they are expected to read the chapters on their own. Having established that expectation early in the semester, it is incumbent upon me to maintain it: if I sometimes teach them everything in a chapter, and sometimes only a few concepts, they will not know how they should study.

With students who are persons of Hispanic origin, you should take advantage of the fact that their culture and their family lives feature peer-to-peer interactivity and teaching (Gutierrez-Clellan, 1999). Because their siblings act as mediators in the home, children and young adults from this minority group are accustomed to learning from each other as much as, if not more than, from the adults in their lives. When learning is modeled by and interpreted by fellow students, they seem to learn better. That is why cooperative learning is consistent with their expectations and intuition, and thus effective for them.

Guideline 3c: Accommodate a wide range of literacy and language skills.

Sciarra and Ponterotto (1991) emphasized the fact that persons of Hispanic origin vary greatly in their receptive and expressive skill with Spanish, as well as with English. Teachers must not assume that they need the same tools and the same accommodations. Some are Spanish-dominant, some truly bilingual, and some actually English-dominant (especially those who are second- or third-generation Americans). Indeed, Sciarra, who is a bilingual counselor, often finds himself translating for parents to their children, and vice versa.

A related point emphasized by Sciarra and Ponterotto is that the cognitive demands of translating from Spanish to English causes many students to concentrate primarily upon how they communicate something (especially in writing), meaning that they have less time to focus upon what they communicate. This has been my experience, as well: my students who are Spanish-dominant require more time to complete tests administered in English than they do to take the same tests in Spanish. I give them that time—it is a reasonable accommodation.

Language Translation

Language translation software is finally coming "of age," so much so that it is now a viable tool for educational use—provided that you call upon a fluent speaker or translator to polish the program's translation. The sheer amount of academic materials (books, articles, etc.) is so vast, and it grows so fast, that without computer-assisted translation, there is little or even no hope of keeping up by producing translated versions. The speed of communication in the classroom presents a very different problem, of course, but one that is also potentially addressable with machine-aided translation.

A big first step has been taken in this field by the Belgian company Lernout & Hauspie (*www.lhsl.com*). Lernout has introduced an affordable language-translation software program, called "L&H Simply Translating[tm] Deluxe," which retails for about $70. It translates English sentences into (and from) Spanish, German, French, Italian, Portuguese, and Japanese. The translations are context-sensitive. Editing by a native speaker of the language is often required, as one might expect, given the maddening peculiarities of languages. Still, the Lernout & Hauspie product greatly speeds up, and simplifies, the important task of making educational materials available in different languages. (Note: The speed with which software evolves is so rapid that by the time you read this Lernout may well have introduced a new version of the program, likely with a new name. However, the company's Web site should offer current information so that you can locate the updated program.)

You will be most likely to find programs that translate between English and Spanish, French, German, Italian, and Japanese. Basic translation software ("basic" meaning that it provides an "initial draft" rather than an exact translation) is free from some sites. Babel Fish (*www.babelfish.altavista.com*) and Transparent Language (*www.freetranslation.com*) both provide no-cost, short-text translations. For-sale versions are better: Transparent Language offers Desktop Translator[tm] for some $100 and Lernout & Hauspie sells Simply Translating[tm] for about $50. Simply Translating[tm] can handle references in 50-some languages, enabling students to get a quick idea of what a passage is about, and can perform much more useful, draft-quality translations between English and a dozen languages. Even these programs are limited in handling poetry and other delicate and refined language (that is, writing in which words are chosen very carefully so as to convey subtle shades of meaning and nuances). Accordingly, use in English literature classes is not recommended; you will have more success with text written in standard business English, as in courses on accounting, education, history, math, research methods, or science. Online, downloadable instant-dictionaries are also available; since they are useful only in translating single words or phrases, they are much more accurate.

Guideline 3d: Arrange information consistent with its importance.

Many people with certain learning disabilities have difficulty organizing information, unless they are given "scaffolding" or some other support, including "advance organizers" that highlight which items of information are particularly important and how these items relate to each other. But all of us benefit when we are helped to identify key data. In this book, each chapter is outlined in the Contents.

PRINCIPLE FOUR: PERCEPTIBLE INFORMATION

Definition: The design communicates necessary information effectively to the user, regardless of ambient conditions or the user's sensory abilities.

Ron Mace and his colleagues wanted to be sure that designers remembered a basic fact: even people whose hearing is unimpaired are, at times, unable to hear well, while people with unimpaired vision often cannot see well enough to read print. They also recognized that there are "eyes busy" or "ears busy" situations in which people cannot focus on additional visual or auditory information. Steps taken to address these temporary needs often help, as well, to meet the needs of people who are deaf or blind.

Learning about perceptibility problems requires a little legwork. My experience is that these become obvious after-the-fact. Gregg Vanderheiden showed me, during a late-1999 trip I made to Madison, Wisconsin, "Visual Eyes"—plastic glasses that simulate low vision (you can see through them, but text and objects appear blurred). These are sold by The Lighthouse (*www.lighthouse.org*). Pharmacies everywhere carry sleeping masks (eyepads) that render you temporarily blind (of course, a scarf tied around the head accomplishes much the same purpose). What I do once outfitted with one of these products is to engage in the activities I expect of my students—getting from a central point on campus to a classroom building, composing text on a computer, and (with Visual Eyes) reading text on a PC screen and in a book. Auditory perceptibility has to be tested by someone else (I am deaf), so I ask a student or an aide to put soft plugs in their ears (these plugs are available at many pharmacies). The plugs limit, but do not prevent, hearing—they simulate hard-of-hearing levels of hearing loss but not deafness. To simulate deafness, it is also necessary for ambient sound to be suppressed (i.e., for people to whisper). With respect to touch sensitivity, simple oven mitts or heavy mittens (not gloves) can simulate quadriplegia or severe arthritis in the hands and fingers. These help in assessing the relative usability of classroom materials and handouts.

Guideline 4a: Use different modes (pictorial, verbal, tactile) for redundant presentation of essential information.

Redundancy

Redundancy is a principle that I championed in the first full-length text about personal computers and people with disabilities (Bowe, 1984). Virtually everything else I wrote in that book is now hopelessly out-of-date, but this one isn't: Information offered in one modality (sound, sight) should be offered, as well, in the other modality. This ensures that people who are deaf can read what people who hear listen to, that people who are blind can listen to what people who see read, and that people with learning disabilities can select the unimpaired modality. Does redundancy also help people with no disabilities? Some recent research suggests that it does. In his review of the literature on this subject, Williams (1998) found that auditory and visual information should be presented simultaneously. Writing in the *Journal of Experimental Psychology*, Tindall-Ford, Chandler, and Sweller (1997) reported on research in which non-disabled participants read text, heard text, and evaluated diagrams. They found that working memory can be enlarged when two senses rather than one are engaged. This makes sense. One fact I committed to memory long ago is that most people can keep in mind only seven (7) discrete pieces of information that they hear in a lecture; this helps me to avoid overloading my students' working memory during lectures. Tindall-Ford *et al.* suggested that this limit may be exceeded if we have access to visual and auditory memory.

Tindall-Ford *et al.* (1997) also found, importantly, that if different information is offered to people visually and auditorially, and they are expected to integrate the visual material with the auditory data, their understanding is slowed significantly. This is something I use in my teaching. As do many professors, I often lecture with the aid of overhead transparencies and/or with Microsoft PowerPoint[R] slides I make a conscious effort to read out loud each word on each transparency or PowerPoint[R] slide. This is sometimes annoying for me, because I have not only already read these materials several times, I wrote them. I must remind myself that for my students they are new. The worst mistake I could make is to show a slide or a transparency and then, without reading it, use it as a springboard to launch into a discussion of what those presentations imply. My students would still be trying to understand the visual message, so they would not be able to process my auditory one.

If you show a video, make every effort to show a captioned one. Captioned videos are widely available today, with thousands more appearing each year, in part because of market forces ("the greying of America" is producing large numbers of older persons with hearing impairment) and in part because of legislation (PL 104-104, the Telecommunications Act of 1996, requires that most new videos, and many older ones as well, be captioned). The "Resources" section that follows Chapter 9 lists the major captioning organizations and companies. They can tell you if a video has already been captioned or, if it has not, they can do the captioning for your school.

Although they are less commonly available, you should seek to find "video–described" tapes and films. Video description is a technique of inserting, where no dialogue or other important sounds occur, narratives that explain what is happening so that blind and low-vision viewers can follow the action. Imagine, for example, that you are watching one of those many television ads that describe a product and then conclude: "Call the number on your screen, right now!" Virtually none of those ads articulates that phone number out loud. As a result, blind viewers have no idea what number to dial.

Video description adds a spoken version of that number. The same principle applies to movies, videos and other presentations: at natural points throughout the story, where sighted but not blind viewers know what is happening, an actor speaks out loud brief descriptions. Thus, in an action movie, the voice might explain: "Rambo is falling off a cliff. Now he lands in a swirling river."

If you use slides, graphs or other audiovisual aids in your teaching, you can video describe them yourself. There is an art to doing this. For pointers, visit *www.wgbh.org/ncam*. That is the National Center for Accessible Media, at WGBH Foundation, in Boston. Their staff includes some of the world's top experts on video description. Briefly: you want to articulate the most salient points of what is being shown, using words to call attention to key features of a slide or graph. As with many other techniques described in this book, you may well find, to your surprise, that doing so also helps sighted students.

Guideline 4b: Maximize "legibility" of essential information.

This is the objective of the eReader^{tm} developed by the Center for Applied Special Technology (CAST). The program, which schools and even students themselves may purchase, gives students control over how information is presented. It adds voice, visual highlighting, document navigation, and other accessibility features to any digital documents—whether scanned-in text, Web pages, word processing files, or text that is typed in by the teacher or student. Thus, students can elect to listen to the text, and can even decide on the volume, pitch, and speed of the voice. They can elect to have text highlighted (to differentiate between letters and symbols that they or their students find confusing or have difficulty telling apart). They can alter the size, font, etc., of displayed text. Students can type in notes while reading, and have those notes spoken back to them upon request. For people who are blind or have low vision, individuals with dyslexia or other learning disabilities, and students for whom English is a second language or a challenge, the eReader^{tm} software makes information more understandable, that is, more legible. It is available for Windows-based PCs and for Macintoshes. (Details: *www.cast.org*.)

Interpreters

For people who are deaf (unable to understand conversational speech through the ear alone, no matter how much amplification is used) or hard of hearing (able to hear and understand some words with the help of a hearing aid or other amplification device), comprehension of essential information can be enhanced in several ways. The first key idea is to offer the same information visually that you present auditorially. An obvious way of doing this is to engage the services of interpreters. Interpreters translate English to American Sign Language (ASL) or some other version of sign, such as pidgin sign language, or even fingerspell everything you and the students say in the classroom. (Fingerspelling is literally "writing in the air": each letter is spelled out on the fingers as it is spoken.) There are a few rules for successful use of interpreters. First, speak directly to your deaf or hard-of-hearing student; do not talk to the interpreter ("Tell him"). Second, do not permit hearing students to engage the interpreter in side conversations; this distracts the interpreter from his or her job. Third, do not accept a deaf or hard-of-hearing student's excuse that he or she did not do well on a test or a paper because of the interpreter. Interpreters are not tutors, nor are they teachers. Their role is strictly limited to transcribing conversational speech in the classroom.

You can also offer deaf or hard-of-hearing students disks or printouts of lectures, write names and technical terms (which are very hard to lipread) on the blackboard or on an overhead transparency when you first speak them, and the like. If the student appears to have particular difficulty keeping up with assigned reading, you may suggest that he or she work with a school tutoring service. Hearing loss that occurs early in life typically limits the extent to which people acquire language in a natural and comprehensive way; difficulty with written English, then, is not indicative of a student's intelligence level, but rather is a predictable consequence of early-onset hearing impairment.

Assistive Listening Systems

Hard-of-hearing, but not deaf, students can benefit from assistive listening systems. A real problem with these otherwise very helpful systems is that every person who wishes to speak must first request the microphone, wait for it, and then speak. This slows down conversation in the classroom. In itself, that's not a bad idea at all, but it does tend to make people with unimpaired hearing rather impatient. At some point in the future, speech recognition may mature to the point that it can be used to produce visible translations of such conversations. However, the fact that people speak very differently means that "speaker independent speech recognition" is going to require enormous computing power, be very expensive (at least in the beginning), and, because it is so complex, be at least five to ten years in the making. Until that day, teachers who have one or more deaf or hard-of-hearing students should ask each student in the class to identify himself or herself before speaking (this enables the person with a hearing loss to know who to lipread), make sure the face is well-lighted (no bright light source behind the head, no shadows on the face), and that no obstructions obscure the view of the hearing-impaired student(s).

Guideline 4c: Differentiate elements in ways that can be described.

As you teach in your classroom, speak out loud every word that you write on the blackboard or that you display using an overhead projector, a PowerPoint[R] slide, or other medium. This provides a way for people who are blind or have low vision to differentiate the scratchings they hear as the chalk moves on the blackboard and the clicking sounds they hear as you click your mouse to activate the PowerPoint^R slides. Otherwise, each chalk sound and each click sounds the same as every other one.

Another example: picture in your mind a Web site you visited recently. In all probability, the screen was filled with hot-link buttons, each programmed to send you automatically to another page or even another site. Now imagine that each one had the same label: "Button." The icons on the buttons are not readable by screen readers (software programs that navigate Web pages and pick out data to be read) and speech synthesizers (hardware and software combinations that read material out loud). Accordingly, such users need a way to distinguish one button from another. A simple mechanism, called "alt text" (for alternative text) is all that is needed: just write a simple description of each particular hotlink (i.e., "Order," "More Information," "Related Sites," etc.), save those descriptions as plain ASCII text, and link them to the button. That way, when the cursor glides over the button, a small "balloon" appears which displays the brief description. Screen readers speak that description out loud. (Details: *www.cast.org*).

Guideline 4d: Provide compatibility with a variety of techniques or devices used by people with sensory limitations.

In education, the term "design" must be broadly interpreted. Consider here the textbook—an ubiquitous feature of education. One exciting option now available to professors and teachers is the digital book (also called "e-book" or electronic book). The number of books offered in digital form is enormous. Barnesandnoble.com *(www.bn.com)* has 2,000 titles in electronic form, for example. The On-Line Books Page (*www.cs.cmu.edu/Web/books.html*) offers some 8,000 texts, some readable while online, plus links to others. The Internet Public Library (*www.ipl.org*) offers links to books, stories, poetry, myths, and magazines. The Etext Archive (*www.etext.org*) has fiction and poetry. The Children's Literature Web Guide *(www.acs.ucalgary.ca/~dkbrown)* offers lesson plans as well as such classics as Lewis Carroll's children's stories. Bookdigital (*www.bookdigital.com*) is a new source, offering e-texts of books and articles that are readable online, as well as links to other sites. These are only a few of the resources now available. Most electronic books to date have been "off copyright" (that is, so old that the copyrights have expired). This is because electronic publishers want to offer a large enough number of titles to attract interest, but to do so at low cost. If the reading public accepts the concept, they expect to be able to offer current titles early in the new century.

Two book "readers" are on the market as this is written: the Rocket eBook^{tm} (about $350) and the SoftBook Reader^{tm} (some $600). The Rocket eBook^{tm} weighs about 1.25 pounds and measures 7 inches high by 5 inches wide by 1 inch deep. It holds some 4,000 pages of text. The SoftBook

Reader[tm] is heavier, at 3 pounds, and larger at 11 inches high by 8.5 inches wide and 1 inch deep. It can hold 100,000 pages of text and grey-scale illustrations. Part of the difference is due to the fact that the Rocket eBook[tm] must be connected to an Internet-ready PC, while the SoftBook Reader[tm] is a stand-alone product. The SoftBookstore *(www.softbook.com)* provides digital newspapers and books to supplement the 100 titles that are included in each SoftBook Reader[tm]. For people who are blind or have dyslexia, Recordings for the Blind & Dyslexic (*www.rfbd.org*) is rapidly converting the 75,000 titles it has in analog (tape) form to digital form. RFB&D (the name was changed in 1995, when the organization belatedly recognized that, even with the old name—Recordings for the Blind, Inc.—67% of their registered users had learning disabilities rather than vision impairments) provides digitized versions of virtually any book or other printed materials that users request. The downside of "E-text" (as RFB&D calls them) is that the voice is synthetic rather than real, as with analog recorded books. Synthesized speech is a computer voice, so it lacks the timber and variety of human speech. Users are willing to put up with speech synthesis because the typical analog recorded book takes up 30 hours of audio tape; those tapes are searchable only by fast-forwarding or rewinding.

An important effort announced in late 1999 was the release of the "Open eBook Publication Structure 1.0" format. Microsoft, Simon & Schuster, and SoftBook Press (a unit of Gemstar[R]), together with other online publishers, acting through The Open eBook Authoring Group, wanted publishers to be able to format books and other materials one time and have that electronic version operate successfully on all devices and using any software. The format is available for review at *www.openebook.org*. For additional information, e-mail *victor.mccrary@nist.gov* (e-mail for Victor McCrary of the National Institute of Technology and Standards, an independent federal agency).

In June 2000, Time Warner[R] took a stake in Bookface.com, an Internet company that enables Web users to read books online. Among other publishers offering the full texts of some of their books are HarperCollins[R], Penguin Putnam[R], St. Martin's Press[R], and TW Trade Publishing[R]. What is interesting about Bookface.com is that visitors to the site can highlight sections of a book, place bookmarks in the text, and take notes, all online.

It did not take long for the idea of e-text to catch on. At the University of Texas at Austin, librarians were startled to discover that some electronic books were being checked out 25 times in just two months. To place that rate into context, they said, consider that the average hard-copy book in their library has a one-in-three chance of ever being checked out (Carvajal, 1999). Why are e-books popular? For one thing, they can be carried around more easily than can a stack of books. As mentioned above, SoftBook Readers[tm] come equipped with 100 classics of literature. Yet the SoftBook Reader[tm] is the size of a trade paperback, as is the Rocket eBook[tm]. For another, search and retrieval is much easier with e-books than with printed books; one simply uses the now-familiar "search" function. This feature can save enormous amounts of time for students who need to write papers about books; it also ensures that the students can locate suitable entries with far greater accuracy. (When she was in college, in the early 1970s, my wife wrote a paper about the houses in Henry James' novels. She had to read each page of each book very carefully! With e-books, every James mention or description of a house is automatically highlighted, making the task much, much easier.)

Another version of electronic publishing has been demonstrated by the Boston-based Center for Applied Special Technology (CAST). If you log onto *www.cast.org* you will find an electronic book about the teaching of reading to K–12 students. This book, *Learning to Read in the Computer Age*, offers excellent formatting—it is really an exemplar of what an e-book should be. Notice especially the hotlinks that are offered throughout the manuscript: each chapter opens with hotlinks to each other chapter, for example, and each chapter concludes with hotlinks to the beginning, end, and other sections of the book. Notice here, too, that hotlinks within the text can transport the reader instantly to sites providing greater detail about ideas being discussed. The entire e-book is, of course, accessible to people who are blind or have dyslexia and depend upon screen readers. CAST is, after all, the originator of the Bobby Web site accessibility checker and the developer of the eReader™ software program for people with learning disabilities.

Electronic texts are most attractive, of course, to people who cannot read printed books—people who are blind and those who have such learning disabilities as dyslexia. Many people who have had a stroke will find them useful, as well. A colleague of mine at Hofstra, special education and gerontology professor Ruth Gold, told me that after her husband had a stroke, reading traditional printed materials was "too much for him and took him so long that he lost sight of the story line." Listening to taped books, however, proved to be a much more agreeable endeavor.

That having been said, do I think e-books will replace printed books at any time in the near future? No, I don't. There is something special about a book, which is why the form has survived for five centuries. I am also acutely conscious that the long-term survivability of electronic media is open to question. I have information on 5.25-inch floppy disks that I can't read any more —not only don't the PCs I have at home and at Hofstra have 5.25-inch disk drives but some of the software used to produce the information is no longer available in any format. Data stored on hard as well as floppy disk drives deteriorates over time. For these reasons, I suggest you take with the proverbial grain of salt the claims of manufacturers that once a book is digitized, it will never go out of print. Besides, I just like the smell and feel of a newly printed book!

Suppose you have a student with low vision in your class. Many such individuals use magnifying devices. How large a type size is appropriate for such uses? I have had good success with black letters of 14 point to 18 point or even larger, printed on white backgrounds. It is easy to prepare using WordPerfect^R or Word^R and an Inkjet^R, DeskJet^R, or similar printer. However, I have had even more success from giving such students a disk: with it, they can enlarge the text to whatever size they prefer and print it out themselves. If they prefer to listen to rather than read print, they can do that, too; in fact, they can convert the text to Braille and read it that way.

If you call or accept calls from students with non-impaired hearing, you should do the same with students who are deaf or hard-of-hearing. This means using, and accepting the students' use of, what are called "dual party relay services." These services are staffed by operators having non-impaired hearing and equipped with TTYs (TDDs) at their work stations. The operator types on the TTY what you say, and speaks out loud what he or she reads on the TTY from the deaf or hard-of-hearing individual. The services are free in all 50 States, thanks to the Americans with Disabilities Act (PL 100-336). Phone numbers are in the White Pages distributed by your local telephone company.

Chapter 6

Principles Five and Six

PRINCIPLE FIVE: TOLERANCE FOR ERROR

Definition: The design minimizes hazards and the adverse consequences of accidental or unintended actions.

Just as a double-cut key may be inserted right-side-up or upside-down, and thus tolerates error (unlike regular keys which must be inserted right-side-up), so, too, does a word-processing program that takes advantage of the "Undo" command in Windows operating systems.

> **Guideline 5a: Arrange elements to minimize hazards and errors: most used elements, most accessible; hazardous elements eliminated, isolated, or shielded.**

Students with arthritis, cerebral palsy, quadriplegia, and other conditions limiting fine-motor control often will benefit considerably from the use of a "keyguard." This is a plastic sheet that fits over a keyboard. The sheet itself offers a resting place for hands and wrists, such that hands do not unintentionally strike keys. Above each key is a hole in the plastic sheet; users insert a finger into that hole to activate the key. This ensures that only the "correct" key is pressed. Keyguards are simple, one-piece products, yet, because relatively few are sold each year, are priced at high levels; your students should expect to pay $100 or even more for a keyguard.

ZoomCaps and other key letters/numbers having larger, more readable characters are readily available from such sources as Maxi Aids (1-800-522-6294) and Flaghouse (1-800-793-7900). They reduce error because people can more easily identify what each key does.

Guideline 5b: Provide warnings of hazards and errors.

Most of my students are required to research and write term papers. I give them a one-pager identifying what I will be looking for in those papers and highlighting mistakes that past students made. I find that this reduces anxiety, because they receive advance warning of what the "hazards" and "errors" are.

Guideline 5c: Provide fail safe features.

I call my students' attention to a feature in Microsoft[R] Word[tm] and Corel[R] WordPerfect[tm]: the Undo command. Although it only undoes the most recent action, I have found it to be very helpful, especially when I am cutting-and-pasting in a manuscript and accidentally move the left margin, which I do quite often. Windows 98[tm] automatically saves the latest version of a document if a power surge or other disaster intervenes before you can save it yourself; I have benefitted from this several times while writing this manuscript.

Error correction takes longer when speech–recognition is being used. Sumh, Myers, and Waibel (1999) studied how people corrected mistakes. Students at Carnegie Mellon University, in Pittsburgh, could fix about three times as many errors by using the keyboard and the mouse as they could by using voice. Lewis (1999), working at IBM, made a similar discovery. When people used the keyboard and mouse in addition to their voices, their "throughput" (a technical term referring to the number of correct words produced per minute) increased. Users could dictate text at a rate of 105 uncorrected words per minute. However, when correcting the inevitable errors, they did much better when allowed to use the keyboard and mouse as well.

Guideline 5d: Discourage unconscious action in tasks that require vigilance.

In this book, I have recommended that teachers consider creating e-mail trees that connect students with each other and with the professor; such listservs facilitate participant interaction between classes. That brings to mind one fail-safe feature I would like to see: a confirmation message that pops up before users broadcast a reply to an e-mail message. Too often, e-mail users automatically "reply" to the entire listserv list when they intended to reply only to the sender of a particular e-mail message. Most readers of this book will recognize the problem. To minimize its occurrence, a simple warning flag could ask: "Do you really want to send this message to all recipients of the original?"

About a week before a term paper is due, I call my students' attention to other features of Word[tm] and WordPerfect[tm]: the spell checker and the grammar checker. I tell them to use those features. I do this because until I began telling them this, I spent an inordinate amount of time flagging misspelled words and ungrammatical sentences in term paper after term paper—all 100% preventible errors. I tell the students that I use the spell checker myself, because I have learned over the years that when I write something, my brain "sees" what I intended to write rather than what I actually wrote. Those experiences have taught me that I cannot proofread my own writing.

PRINCIPLE SIX: LOW PHYSICAL EFFORT

Definition: The design can be used efficiently and comfortably and with a minimum of fatigue.

Lever handles on doors were originally designed to facilitate operation by people who have quadriplegia, cerebral palsy, arthritis, or other conditions limiting fine-motor control.

Guideline 6a: Allow user to maintain a neutral body position.

Moveable desks and chairs allow students to sit as close to each other, or as far away, as they find comfortable. As noted in Chapter 1, "personal space" may differ significantly, depending upon culture. Moveable desks and chairs also allow students to place personal-use accessibility items, such as crutches, near them, yet out of the way so that they do not interfere with the mobility of other students.

Guideline 6b: Use reasonable operating forces.

Doors are particularly difficult for many people to open—unnecessarily so. The amount of pressure required to open most doors is adjustable. If a student of yours has difficulty, consult with the school's facilities staff. In addition, levers (instead of door knobs) make opening doors much easier—for most everyone.

Guideline 6c: Minimize repetitive actions.

An obvious example: reduce the number of times a student with a physical disability must traverse between floors, or between buildings. If all or most of his or her classes can reasonably be located on one floor, this should be done. The sheer amount of physical effort, not to mention time, required for people who walk with mobility aids or who use manual wheelchairs has to be experienced to be appreciated. (I have assigned students to "spend a weekend in a wheelchair," after which they routinely make two observations: one, everything takes so much longer (from dressing to eating to traveling), and two, they really appreciate the need for upper-body strength after pushing that wheelchair for two or three days!

Guideline 6d: Minimize sustained physical effort.

Distance Learning

Done correctly, distance learning offers an equivalent learning experience for people who have severe physical or health conditions as for individuals for whom travel to and from class is inconvenient or temporarily impossible. That is why distance learning has appealed so strongly to women (many of whom are mothers of young children), career-changers (people looking for new challenges while still doing their current jobs), teachers seeking additional credits so as to become certified by state education agencies, and others for whom time is valuable. It also has obvious appeal for people who reside in rural areas for whom the option of in-person university courses does not exist.

Distance learning is now in its fourth generation (Dirr, 1999). The first was "correspondence education," through which student and professor exchanged what we now call "snail mail." That began, in the United States, in the 1800s. The second, in the 1950s, used television to deliver instruction; a well-known example was "Sunrise Semester." The third, in the late 1980s, used the then-infant Internet (ARPANET) to offer online courses to scientists and engineers affiliated with universities and research centers. The fourth, beginning in the 1990s, features a wide range of computer-based programming, ranging from listservs and e-mail all the way to two-way multimedia virtual classrooms, in which students at remote locations see and hear everything they would were they physically in the classroom with the instructor. We even have a journal dedicated to the topic, *The American Journal of Distance Education.*

As practiced early in the new century, distance learning is either *synchronous* (real-time, with scheduled meeting times), with interactive video conferencing being a popular example, or *asynchronous* (virtual time, with no scheduled meeting periods), as illustrated by virtual classrooms, in which instructors post materials on a Web page, where they are retrieved at convenient times by students, usually working from home, and responded to (including completed assignments) via email. Distance learning appeals primarily to people for whom traditional instruction is inconvenient or actually impossible. To illustrate, Bremner (1998) reports that some 68% of distance learning students are female and that 80% of those women have young children; distance learning is also popular with teachers and other professionals seeking re-certification. Both groups have a strong interest in avoiding weekly commutes to a university for a 15-week semester. Of course, for the same reasons, distance learning also serves people with severe physical disabilities or health conditions that make travel impossible, and persons with other limitations who find some such travel to be nearly so (e.g., a user of a power wheelchair who cannot get out of the house due to a heavy snowfall). Thus, distance learning is an example of universal design—the same features that meet special needs can respond to convenience needs of the general population.

For students, the distance learning experience is not identical to the in-person one, but it is comparable. When they can enroll in and "attend" classes from remote locations, even from their living rooms, they may actually enjoy benefits not realized by in-person students. That is because people can tap adaptive equipment they have in their homes or offices. It is also because the technology required to connect distance-learning students and the professor/st·`dents on site lends itself readily to such adaptations. Take, for example, e-mail. Distance learning courses typically make very heavy use of e-mail, far more than do most in-person courses. This means that technology can enhance the accessibility of the course for all students, even for those who sit in the classroom. Students send questions and professors reply with answers via e-mail systems. Students may also attach term papers to e-mail messages. By distributing course materials through e-mail rather than (or in addition to) on paper, professors give students options on how to "read" the information. If the student is blind or has dyslexia, it is a simple matter for him or her to listen to a speech synthesizer articulate the material aurally. Students may also research papers using the World Wide Web or other Internet resources such as "gopher" (a text-based information retrieval system developed at the University of Minnesota which presents choices in list form, with each option accompanied by a number). Again, the information is offered electronically and may be listened to rather than read. Distance learning can also be provided in a form that stresses independent study by students rather than the traditional lecture-and-note-taking format. Such approaches may appeal to older learners as well as to students with some kinds of learning disabilities.

It is urgently important that distance-learning offerings are usable by people with different needs. Stuart Skorman, the founder of Reel.com, a company that was acquired by Hollywood Video in 1999, knew this from personal experience. Remembering his own college experiences as a student who had learning disabilities as well as attention deficit disorders, Skorman created Hungry Minds™, a Web site focused on providing online college courses that anyone can use. He forged agreements with the University of California at Berkeley, the University of Maryland, and others to offer courses ranging from computer skills to literature. That is why I was disappointed to discover that the HungryMinds™ Web site was not accessible to people who use screen readers, which many people with dyslexia and other learning disabilities do. (I immediately alerted the HungryMinds™ Webmaster and asked him to visit the "Bobby" web site checker [*www.cast.org/bobby*] to request assistance.) Anticipating that the rather modest changes needed are in fact made, this site is worth visiting as it offers thousands of online courses. (Details: *www.hungryminds.com.*) The point is central: when universally designed, distance learning enhances education for all students.

The words "sustained physical effort" can also apply to less obvious situations. My classes last nearly two hours. I have found that my students, most of whom work during the day and attend my courses at night, greatly appreciate it when I break up the lecture, so they get opportunities to become physically active. Similarly, when I give them manipulatives and engage them in role-playing (as when they don special glasses that simulate low vision or wear mufflers to simulate hearing loss) or in exercises (trying to lipread each other, going to the rest room while blindfolded), they find that the time passes much faster.

Many of my students enjoy opportunities to engage in small-group discussions and to work as team members on term projects. These are also examples of reducing students' perceptions of "sustained physical effort" because, for these students at least, the work seems less onerous.

Chapter 7

Principle Seven

PRINCIPLE SEVEN: SIZE AND SPACE FOR APPROACH AND USE

Definition: Appropriate size and space is provided for approach, reach, manipulation, and use regardless of user's body size, posture, or mobility.

The issues in Principle Seven are much more obviously applicable to building design than to education. However, they do have implications for teachers. These are explored below.

Accessibility in the built environment has been a requirement in the United States for more than 25 years. In 1973, the Rehabilitation Act (PL 93-112) created the U.S. Architectural and Transportation Barriers Compliance Board ("Access Board") and gave it responsibility for enforcing the 1968 Architectural Barriers Act, which required that many buildings constructed by federal agencies be accessible to and usable by people with disabilities. The Board began doing so in 1975. Even before that time, the American National Standards Institute (ANSI) had published a voluntary set of guidelines, still known as ANSI A117.1. Over time, the Access Board's rules, which have become mandatory for public and private entities subject to the Rehabilitation Act and the Americans with Disabilities Act of 1990 (ADA; PL 101-336), and ANSI's A117.1 voluntary guidelines have become more similar. The ANSI A117.1 standard is available from the Institute (details: *www.ansi.org*).

In late 1999, the Access Board published a set of proposed changes to its 1991 ADA Accessibility Guidelines for Buildings and Facilities (ADAAG) *(Federal Register*, November 16, 1999). When the changes become final in late 2000, they will serve as a minimum baseline for federal agencies that enforce the ADA, notably including the U.S. Department of Justice. The Access Board itself, and its Guidelines, have no statutory authority over most buildings and facilities. The Justice Department adopted the 1991 ADAAG and made it enforceable; I expect Justice to do the same with the 1999 revisions. For updates, see the Access Board's Web site (*www.access-board.gov*) and that of the Justice Department (*www.usdoj.gov*).

The ADAAG offers very specific guidance (e.g., how wide, how high) and applicability ("scoping"—how many of each kind of feature) standards. For example, college campuses have large parking lots ("large" being a relative term: as one wag put it, "A university is a community of scholars united by the search for a parking space!"). The ADAAG explains what dimensions a "handicapped parking space" must have and how many such spaces are required in parking lots of various sizes. Similarly, some classroom buildings have banks of pay phones. The ADAAG notes how some of those phones should be equipped with volume controls and how many phones in each phone bank must have such controls. In general, these specifications and scoping requirements apply to new buildings and to newly renovated parts of existing buildings; some, however, apply to non-renovated sections of existing buildings.

The major elements to look for in the 2000 revision of the ADAAG include a new numbering system that will make the guidelines more easily compared to model building codes and industry standards such as the ANSI A117.1 guidelines; new specifications on clear floor space, turnaround room, knee and toe clearances, and operable parts; accessible route changes, including materials for exterior paths and children's playground areas; new rules on alarms and alarm systems, signs, telephones, two-way communication systems, and interactive transaction machines like kiosks that students use to check course schedules and their grades. There may also be new guidelines on fixed furnishings, which may be relevant to high-school and college laboratories.

Chapter 11 of the new guidelines will include materials relating to college dormitory buildings and dorm rooms. Until the revisions are published, educators may benefit from "5 Steps to Make New Lodging Facilities Comply with the ADA" (*www.usdoj.gov/crt/ada/fivestep.htm*). Newly constructed or newly renovated dormitory buildings and rooms ("new" defined as designed and constructed after January 26, 1993, the date title III of the Americans with Disabilities Act became effective, need to comply with the ADA. Also helpful are "Common ADA Problems at Newly Constructed Lodging Facilities" and "ADA Checklist for Newly Constructed Lodging Facilities," both of which are available at the Justice website. In general, doors should allow 32 inches of clear entrance/exit space, meaning that most doorways should be 36 inches or more wide (to allow for hinges, etc.). The only exception is for shallow closet doors. Doors and in-room controls (temperature, etc.) should feature levers and other easily grasped and readily operated controls. About four (4) rooms per 100 in a dormitory should be equipped with visual (flashing) alarms. Roll-in showers, equipped with folding seats, are required for a certain proportion of dorm rooms. In general, a dormitory having 50 dorm rooms should have two (2) roll-in shower stalls, appropriately located adjacent to accessible dorm rooms. The parking lot near the dormitory room should have three (3) handicapped parking spaces plus one extra-large van parking space per 100 rooms. (The required number of such spaces is lower for the second 100 rooms and then for the third 100 rooms, but relatively few dormitories have more than 100 rooms.)

In 1998, the Access Board released an addendum to the ADAAG called "Building Elements Designed for Children's Use" (details: *www.access-board.gov*). These "children's standards" provide specifications for new and newly renovated parts of existing buildings that primarily or largely serve children aged 2–12. If your school serves such children, you may want to alert facilities managers to such issues as door pressure (how easily doors open), height of drinking fountains, layout and dimension of rest rooms, and the like: these may differ significantly from guidelines that apply to buildings used primarily by adults.

For information about physical design features, consult the multimedia instructional program, "Designing Accessible Environments," available from the IDEA Center, University at Buffalo. It is distributed on 3.5-inch disks and requires the user to have an Intel 80486 processor (or a more powerful one, such as a Pentium), at least 10 MB of hard-drive space, 8 MB of free memory, and 16-bit graphics. (Details: *www.ap.buffalo.edu/~idea*). Other resources include the Center for Universal Design (*www.design.ncsu.edu/cud*) and Adaptive Environments (*www.adaptenv.org*).

Guideline 7a: Provide a clear line of sight to important elements for any seated or standing user.

There is a variation on "clear line of sight" that has personal meaning for me. When I was in college, in the late 1960s, I had professors who sometimes sat on window sills on sunny days. The bright light behind them cast their faces into shadow. Of course, that made lipreading impossible. I would hope no teacher today would be that insensitive. Many of us do something almost as bad, however: we talk while we are writing on the blackboard, or while we are writing on an overhead transparency (looking down). In both instances, someone who depends on lipreading misses out. Educators need to remind themselves that today's noisy environments and extremely loud rock concerts have produced sizeable hearing impairments in large numbers of students. Some people who have learning disabilities also depend, to some extent, upon lipreading, even if they are not aware of doing so. So do many other individuals (have you ever heard someone say, "I hear so much better with my glasses on"?). For each of these needs, a simple mental note ("Face the class when talking") is all the teacher needs.

A related issue is that of classroom acoustics. People who should know tell me that the acoustics of the average classroom are really poor. In fact, I'm told that some students can't hear as many as one-third of the words teachers speak in classrooms. There are no national standards for classroom acoustics.

Ceilings are important; to upgrade them so as to enhance sound transmission costs about 13 cents per square foot. Also important is sound-absorbing treatment for walls and floors (Lubman, 1999). ANSI, through its S12 Committee's Working Group 42, is drafting standards (details: *www.ansi.org*) and the Access Board is also looking into this area (details: *www.access-board.gov*). Meanwhile, there are steps educators can take. One was suggested by a student of mine. She told me that she has "looped" her room for FM technology. She wears a small microphone on a headset. The words she speaks into that microphone are broadcast to her students through four speakers placed around the room. (FM technology, as well as the related AM and infrared technologies, usually transmit signals to "receivers" [sort of like hearing aids] that are worn by particular students.) She told me that her students, all of whom have unimpaired hearing, have greatly benefitted from this.

Most classroom buildings have alarm systems. The Access Board's guidelines specify that, in new buildings and in newly constructed parts of existing buildings, audible alarms should be accompanied by visual alarms. The intent is to be common-sense about this: As a deaf person, I will know immediately if an audible alarm sounds simply because the hearing people around me will react to it; accordingly, as long as I am with such individuals, I do not require a visual alarm. However, when and where I am not, I do. Hence, these rules apply to common areas where people who are deaf may be isolated or alone. A good example is rest rooms. Adding visual to audible alarms when alarm systems are initially installed raises costs by about $250 per alarm unit. However, in existing buildings where audible but not visual alarms are in place, adding new visual signalers can be much more expensive. The Access Board recommends that facilities managers consider whether a few strategically placed visual alarms will suffice, so as to contain costs.

On any large campus, such as Hofstra's, signage is extremely important. On any given day, several hundred people not familiar with the university's layout visit Hofstra. This raises questions about signs. First, we need to examine external maps and signs. The general rule is that signs should be readable by people with some residual vision—this means high contrast (black ink on white background or vice versa). Readability is enhanced when signs are at eye level: no more than 48 inches and no less than 35 inches from the ground. It is also improved when the sign is actually touchable. If so, it should have raised or indented (raised are preferable) letters, numbers, and/or features so that people who are blind can read it with their fingers. I do not recommend Braille on such signs, because only about 10% of people who are blind even know Braille; but if adding Braille can be accomplished without much difficulty or expense, that should be done: the Access Board insists in its Accessibility Guidelines that new building signs intended to be within touch range feature Grade II Braille. Raised or indented characters and Brailling are obviously pointless in maps or signs that are not intended to be touched.

External building signs are also important. At Hofstra, most of our classroom buildings are named only in very large lettering that is chiseled above the second-floor level. While this is helpful for people who know where to look, my experience is that additional signage is needed. (Virtually every day, I am asked by visitors where some building or other is located.) Highly visible signage placed between 35 inches and 60 inches above ground level, with most lettering centered at around 48 inches from ground level, and situated on at least one corner of a building would, I believe, greatly assist newcomers in locating buildings. I like corner signs, because they can be seen from several directions, thus attracting the attention of people who wish to come closer to read them. If placed on every public-use building on campus, these signs would become prominent enough that even first-time visitors would quickly learn where to look for them.

Guideline 7b: Make reach to all components comfortable for any seated or standing user.

To follow this guideline, people need to know what maximum reach heights are. That is, how far from the floor may a control, or switch, or knob be and still be usable by someone in a wheelchair? According to the Access Board, forward reach for a person with a wheelchair is a maximum of 48 inches (measured from the floor); side reach is 54 inches. However, the Board notes in its November 16, 1999, proposed rule-making on the Accessibility Guidelines that a side reach limit of 48 inches is more realistic, particularly for little people (dwarfs). Little people generally are under 4 feet 10 inches tall. If controls, keys, et cetera, may be up to 48 inches above floor level, what about the minimum heights? The Access Board suggests 35 inches as that standard—below that level, people using wheelchairs may tip over attempting to reach low-lying electrical outlets or other controls/switches. These height levels are critically important for kiosks, including machines where students check course schedules, grades, et cetera.

These dimensions obviously apply to adults rather than to children. If the facility serves children aged 2–12, then the maximum reach heights (again, from the floor) should be about 36 inches (for preschoolers) to 44 inches (for 9–12 year-olds). *Minimum* reach heights (once again, as measured from the floor) should be some 20 inches (preschoolers) to 16 inches (9–12 year-olds). The latter numbers may seem to be counter-intuitive. Consider them, however, from the point of view of someone sitting in a wheelchair. The bigger the student, the less the downward reach ability without risking a fall out of the chair. These dimensions apply not only to PCs and related furnishings but also to light switches, electrical wall outlets, automatic door opening controls, and other items people are expected to touch. The general idea is to make them high enough so that tipping over from the wheelchair is not a danger, yet low enough so that they may safely be reached from a seated position.

Students also need to be able to sit comfortably and to have ready access to paper, books, pens, etc. I had a student in Spring 1999 who was well into her pregnancy. She could not use the standard-issue desks/chairs in the classroom. I arranged for building custodians to provide her with a portable desk, about half the size of my own, and a moveable chair. That was all she needed.

This guideline also applies to the larger dimensions of schools and classrooms. In general, hallways between classrooms should be a minimum of 44 inches wide. This is true whether the primary users are young children or full-grown adults. That is because young children generally do not have the fine-motor control and dexterity that adults have; they simply need more room to move because they are much less able to maintain a straight path of travel. Ideally, halls should be some 88 inches wide, which is the minimum width needed for two wheelchair users to pass each other, whether going in the same or the opposite direction.

Guideline 7c: Accommodate variations in hand and grip size.

Here is a neat example of universal design at work: door levers instead of door knobs. Hofstra's Breslin Hall is a relatively new classroom building in which I have many of my classes. In 1998, I asked the university to replace the door knobs with levers. I did that because I found it annoying to have to put down the briefcase, handouts, etc., that I carried to class in order to open classroom doors. After a brief argument ("It will cost us about $16,000 to do that!") the university complied with my request. Now I simply bump the lever with an elbow (or with my rear end) and the door opens. Levers were initially introduced as door openers that people with quadriplegia or other fine-motor control limitations could use much easier than they can door knobs. I don't have any such restrictions. But when I carry things in both hands, I do—and I benefit from the same accessibility features.

One student I taught in Fall 1999 was a little person. He stood well under 4 feet tall. As is common with little people (dwarfs), his fingers were large proportionate to his hands. He needed an extra-large (note: not, as one might have imagined, small) pen to write with. These are readily available. Wide-grip holders are sold in many K-Mart, Williams Sonoma, and Walmart stores and even in some Home Depot stores, which may be used to hold a wide variety of items.

Guideline 7d: Provide adequate space for the use of assistive devices or personal assistance.

A clear path for a wheelchair into and around the room is an obvious example; too many classrooms have desks scattered around the room, including right in front of the door. With moveable desks, I can easily clear out an accessible path within minutes of arriving in the classroom, thus facilitating movement by students who use wheelchairs. With fixed desks, the maneuverability of these people is unnecessarily limited, usually to one part of the room.

Desks and other writing surfaces should provide sufficient space under the surface for the legs of people using wheelchairs. With adults, this generally means knee and toe clearance dimensions of about 27 inches from floor to the bottom of the writing surface, about 19 inches from the edge of the writing surface to the farthest key or control the person is expected to reach and operate with fingers, and some 30 inches from the right edge of the writing surface to the left edge (that is, the writing surface area). With children aged 2–12, the knee and toe clearance area beneath the writing surface should be about 24 inches and the farthest control about 14 inches from the edge of the writing surface; the width of the writing surface should be some 30 inches, as with adults.

Edward Steinfeld, professor of architecture and head of the IDEA Center at the State University at Buffalo, in upstate New York, has observed that while we generally think of larger, wide-open spaces when we talk about "accessibility," in actuality smaller distances can reduce students' expenditure of energy. He spoke at the Sixth Ibero-American Conference on Accessibility, June 19, 1994, in Rio De Janeiro (see *www.ap.buffalo.edu/~idea* for the text of his speech). This is a good example of how universal design forces even experts on accessibility, which Steinfeld certainly is, to reconsider "obvious" ideas. Knowing that older persons and people using wheelchairs or other mobility devices have enrolled in a class of mine, I can work with the university's classroom scheduling staff members to identify an available classroom that is close to drop-off sites of public buses (and, at Hofstra, of the campus "Blue Beetle" buses) and to parking lots featuring a good number of handicapped parking spaces. I can also request a room near the main entrance of the building, on the first floor, et cetera. All of these location characteristics reduce the physical effort my students will need to expend. Within the room itself, Steinfeld noted, we should reduce the amount of bending and stretching required. A simple example is electrical outlets. When my students bring a laptop to class to use in a presentation, they can plug it into the wall much more easily if an outlet is at least 18 inches above floor level than, as is usually the case, just 9 inches to 12 inches from the floor.

It is important, too, to recognize that what children and adults consider to be "adequate space" may vary by culture. People of some non-European cultures may like to be closer together, while some from northern European cultures may be distinctly uncomfortable unless they have much more personal space. People who are blind, and a few who are deaf, use guide dogs; room should be available for those dogs to sit near their owners yet not obstruct the passage of other individuals. Finally, a minimum of five feet of unobstructed "turnaround space" is needed in rest rooms and classrooms so that people using wheelchairs can manipulate the chair safely and effectively. Room doorways should be at least 36 inches wide, which is what is needed for an effective 32-inch opening (after accounting for the width of the door and hinges).

Many students with cerebral palsy and some who have quadriplegia need a personal assistant who writes for them; other students, who are blind or have learning disabilities, also need an assistant when taking a test. What I have usually done is to arrange for these students to take the test in a different location, often at a different time, to avoid distracting other students. However, that is not a concern during regular class sessions, so we just permit the writer to sit beside the student needing assistance.

Chapter 8

Web Site Accessibility

Increasingly, teachers are using course and personal Web sites for instructional purposes. This raises an important question: How can we ensure that Web sites, and the pages comprising them, are accessible to diverse users? There is a legal aspect to this issue: the Americans with Disabilities Act (PL 101-336) requires colleges, universities, and continuing and adult education programs (referred to in the Act's title III as "places of public accommodation") to ensure that Web sites these educational institutions use to communicate with their students and prospective students are accessible and usable by people with disabilities. This interpretation of title III originated in a letter sent by U.S. Senator Tom Harkin (a chief Senate sponsor of the law) to the U.S. Department of Justice, and in a reply sent to Senator Harkin by Deval Patrick, Assistant Attorney General for Civil Rights (see *National Disability Law Reporter*, *10*(6), September 11, 1997). In this exchange of letters, key representatives of the legislative and executive branches of the federal government agreed that when places of public accommodation use the Internet, including the World Wide Web, to communicate with members of their publics, they must make sure that these accommodate the needs of people with disabilities.

YOUR OWN WEB PAGES

There are several rules to follow—fortunately, they are simple ones. An excellent resource is the World Wide Web Consortium (W3C), an international working group with impressive support from government and industry alike. W3C's Web Accessibility Initiative (WAI), under the leadership of Judy Brewer, has developed resources that you can use. These include:

Quick Tips ("business-card sized" highlights)

Web Content Accessibility Guidelines (includes checkpoints, techniques, a fact sheet, and a curriculum teaching the guidelines and techniques)

Authoring Tool Accessibility Guidelines
Policies Related to Web Accessibility
Reference List on Web Accessibility

The uniform resource locator (URL) is: *www.w3.org/WAI/*. You may also send questions to: *wai@w3.org*.

In general, you should not add bells, whistles, and frills that are not needed. A good introduction to these issues was offered by *Wired* magazine in late 1999. Matt Margolin wrote a three-part tutorial on how to make Web sites more user-friendly. Lesson 1 examined the relevant laws. In Lesson 2, Margolin discussed links and coding. In Lesson 3, he offered style sheets. (*www.hotwired.com/webmonkey/html/tutorials/tutorial1.html.*)

First, add text descriptions to graphics, icons, and similar symbols. These kinds of images can help visitors who are mentally retarded or have some learning disabilities. However, they need an "add on" because images cannot be read by "screen readers." Screen readers are software programs that navigate screens and convert information so that it can be spoken aloud by speech synthesizers (the hardware and software programs that actually do the speaking). To make information accessible to screen-readers, images must be accompanied by screen reader text, known as alt text (for "alternative text"). Alt text is a simple text file that describes the graphic or the icon. For example, my Web page at Hofstra (*http://people.hofstra.edu/faculty/frank_g_bowe*) has photos of the covers of some of my books. Each cover has an accompanying text file. I also have an alt text for my picture, identified by a "d" to the right of the photograph. Users clicking on the "d" find a brief, two-sentence description of the picture (telling them that it is a photo of me standing in front of the Capitol in Washington, DC).

Second, try not to use tables for layout. Many tables are designed to be read column–by–column, that is, vertically. To understand the problems tables pose, bear in mind that screen readers navigate horizontally from the left side of the screen to the right. They do this whether or not the result makes any sense. Consider the example of Table 8.1. Here is what you would actually hear spoken aloud: "Table 1. Week. Apples Sold. Cumulative Totals. 1. 25. 25. 2. 10. 35." It should be evident that this presents a cognitive load on the user. While that load is bearable in this example, it may well not be with more detailed or complicated tables. What should you do? Present the information in a horizontally readable table, or (if it is a very simple and short table) offer the information in narrative form—that is, in sentences that can be read. ("In Week 1, 25 apples were sold. The second week, another 10 were sold, bringing the total to 35 apples.")

Table 8.1

Week	Apples Sold	Cumulative Totals
1	25	25
2	10	35
3	40	75
4	25	100

"Frames," pull-down menus that function independently of the background Web page, are OK. They let users scroll down a small menu on the left side (or the right) of a screen, until a desired entry is located, which is then highlighted and clicked. These used to be a very big problem for users of screen readers (Margolin, 1999), but most such users have learned how to deal with frames.

Third, avoid unnecessary clutter. Today, you have humongous numbers of options, including dancing nuns, exploding firecrackers, and wallpaper-type background colors. Ignore them. If you look at my Web page, for example, you will see plain white backgrounds; that is because black text on white backgrounds is easily read by people with vision impairments and many with learning disabilities. You will also see no moving images at all.

If the Web pages you use for your course follow the above three suggestions, submit them to "Bobby" for evaluation. Bobby is an automated Web-page access checker created by the Center for Applied Special Technology (CAST). If Bobby approves a page as accessible, it signals this by displaying blue hardhats. (The name "Bobby" comes from that of a British police officer.) If your pages are approved, you are also permitted to insert the "Bobby Approved" symbol on your Web page. The Web address (uniform resource locator [URL]) for Bobby is: *www.cast.org/bobby*.

Fourth, Margolin suggested, offer visitors the option, at the top of the first Web page, of choosing a "text version" of your site. This is no longer recommended by the W3 WAI group. Text versions are ASCII-based, graphics-free variations of the same information. They are very easy for screen readers to navigate. However, reality is that people update the "main" site far more often than they do the "text version," leaving screen reader users behind. Another reason, still valid, for using text versions is that they are rapidly loaded, thus avoiding the "World Wide Wait" that so many users find annoying. All you need to do is to create a different file for each Web page, keeping this one free of any formatting, graphics, etc., and to save the result as plain ASCII or plain HTML. (Note that text versions will not include images that you use to hotlink visitors to other Web sites. Users of screen readers will not get the hotlink at all, so of course they won't be able to use it as you intended. This is why hotlinks should be text, not images.)

Fifth, consider offering visitors the option of selecting popular languages other than English. Spanish, Portuguese, French, and German are especially suitable options. (You may wish to use Lernout & Hauspie's language translation programs to produce the initial drafts of these options [*www.lhsl.com*] and then having a colleague who is fluent in the target language polish the text.)

Sixth, follow common-sense guidelines. Make all pages at your site "look similar" in some way (i.e., with standard layouts, similar colors, identifying text and icons). This is because many people with learning disabilities become confused when navigating between sites that are hotlinked; they need something on the screen that tells them "where" they are. Provide simple navigation tools, notably a way to return to the main page, a link at the bottom of each page allowing the user to return quickly to the top of that page, and the like. Outstanding examples are offered at CAST's Web site. Note, especially, the use of tabs at the tops of Web pages that link to other sections; these function like the tabs provided in notebook section dividers.

Finally, if appealing to older adults is one of your goals, visit Microsoft's Web page to review its "White Paper" on Web design and seniors (*www.microsoft.com/seniors*). One suggestion: increase contrast between content and background. This is because people's vision naturally deteriorates with age, making it more difficult for older than for younger people to distinguish between colors. That is why black-on-white or white-on-black is far superior to black-on-grey or brown-on-tan layouts. For the same reason, small blocks of text surrounded by large amounts of white space increase readability. Microsoft hints that a simple test of readability is to hold a piece of yellow cellophane in front of your eyes to simulate age-related visual impairment. Another is to view your Web page on a black-and-white monitor (rather than a color monitor)—you may be very surprised how different your Web page looks! As these ideas imply, the guidance offered elsewhere in this chapter (intended to enhance accessibility for people who have disabilities) are directly applicable to making Web pages more usable by senior citizens.

One that is somewhat different is to consider designing your Web site so that it offers "pages" that stand alone, rather than "pages" that require users to scroll line-by-line and overflow from one screen to another. Research reported at a recent meeting of the Human Factors and Ergonomics Society suggests that older persons who are new to the Web do much better when they encounter "pages" that are one screen in size. Mead, Spaulding, Sit, Meyer, and Walker (1997) asked persons having little experience navigating the Web to conduct searches at different Web sites. Young adults (19–36 years of age) were compared to older adults (64–81 years of age). The older users were much more likely to search "one page at a time" and less successful when they had to click three or more times to navigate between "pages" on Web sites. According to the researchers, the key problem apparently is one of memory—viewing sites one page at a time imposed lower cognitive burdens than did viewing sites one line at a time while scrolling among multiple screens.

Here are some other ideas offered by the W3C's Web Accessibility Initiative: provide captions for video and transcripts for audio that is offered at your Web site. Hotlinks should be understandable if read in isolation (e.g., out of context); thus, you should avoid hotlinks like "Click here" and favor hotlinks like "For more information about this course, click here." (This is because screen readers may not advise users about the contexts in which hotlinks appear on the screen; the purpose of the hotlink will be evident to sighted visitors, but may not be to blind visitors.) The WAI group suggests that you use the tools and guidelines they offer: *www.w3.org/TR/WAI-WEBCONTENT*.

In all you do, bear in mind that the guiding principle is to make your Web site easily readable, easily navigable, and informative and useful. It is not to impress students and other visitors with your "artiness" and creativity.

ACCESS TO OTHER PEOPLE'S WEB PAGES

Several million Web pages are reachable by anyone served by an Internet Service Provider (ISP). The vast majority are not fully accessible to people who use screen readers or who cannot read English. If such pages are important for your students to visit, this is a real problem.

Perhaps the first issue to address is a basic one: people who are blind and many who have low vision or dyslexia can make only limited use of today's highly graphical Web browsers, such as Netscape Navigator. Making matters worse is the fact that most Web sites that these browsers reach are also highly graphical. I find myself using an old standby: LYNX. This is a text-only browser. A variation on LYNX comes from an unexpected source: the National Aeronautics & Space Administration (NASA). NASA developed Iliad, a text-based search tool. (The name is an acronym: Internet Library Information Access Device.) Here's how it works. A user sends an e-mail message to: *iliad@msstate.edu*, or to *iliad@prime.jsc.nasa.gov*, or to *iliad@rosy.tenet.edu*. The user leaves the "Subject" line blank. In the body of the e-mail message, the user types (without the quotes): "start iliad." A return e-mail will be sent, asking the user to specify the information being sought and the Web site(s) where it may reside. About half an hour later, Iliad replies with a plain-text e-mail containing the desired information. Iliad ignores highly graphical material (Williams, 1999). For this reason, if the information you want your students to acquire is found only in graphical form, you will probably need to take a different tack. Iliad returns only text materials, ignoring any icons, graphics, etc., that are not described with alt text or long descriptions (longdesc).

You may have to visit a Web site yourself, extract the essential information, and post it yourself, in accessible form, giving credit to the source. Of course, if you want to download the material directly, you must first request permission. Another step is for you, or the student, to send an e-mail message to the offending Webmaster. (Most Web pages make this easy, by offering you a hotlink that automatically creates and addresses an e-mail message to the page's creator.) Explain briefly that the site is not accessible, recommend Bobby, and request changes. That should suffice in some cases. I use this method and find that, in general, Webmasters reply within a week to two weeks, acknowledging the problem; they take as many as six months, however, to fix it, if indeed they do.

Regardless of the outcome of such efforts, there are some basic things that students can do. One is for speech synthesis hardware and software to be implemented at the student's PC. Apple's Macintosh machines, including the new iMacs, talk—they have built-in speech synthesis capabilities, and have for many years. Users simply have to "call up" the program, that is, to deploy it (details: *www.speech.apple.com*). With PCs, separate hardware and software generally is required. With respect to hardware, the important elements are *sound cards and speakers*. Speakers are common peripherals that are provided with PCs at no extra cost. Sound cards, however, usually have to be purchased separately. Sound cards convert digital information to analog form. The better the sound card, the clearer the speech. My experience is that people who use speech synthesis on a daily basis quickly become accustomed to the artificial voices, even if they are not of high quality. People who use speech synthesis only upon occasion, however, need a good sound card. That is because it can require days, even weeks, to become used to the speech produced by low-cost synthesizers.

In addition, software is needed. What screen reader software does is to navigate the screen, select what is to be read, etc. The user determines whether the synthesizer should articulate punctuation (i.e., call out "comma"), spell unfamiliar words, and the like. The user also sets the rate of speed of the voice. Good software also gives the user a choice of voices—a male, a female, a child, a person with a Spanish accent, etc. This can be very important for young children if they use this voice to speak on their behalf (i.e., if they have cerebral palsy or are deaf).

IBM's Via Voice[tm] Millennium software program, introduced in late 1999, has three components. Via Voice[tm] Web allows users to open Web pages by speaking to the computer; in fact, users can assign numbers to often-visited sites and call up a particular site simply by saying "Number Seven." Via Voice[tm] Standard lets people dictate text into a basic word processor; this is helpful for notes and short messages. Via Voice[tm] Pro lets people dictate text and format it using programs such as Microsoft[R] Word[tm]. One feature of Via Voice[tm] Millennium is a "personal agent" that allows users to dictate e-mail messages. The product is available both for PCs and for iMacs. For more information, contact IBM at *www.ibm.com*.

If your student has low vision, he or she may be able to benefit from the screen enlargement feature that is included in most PCs and Macs. (Look under "Settings," then "Control Panel," and then—depending on the operating system —"Accessibility Features" or "Display.") Generally, magnification of up to 16 times is offered. If greater enlargement is needed, the student must acquire off-the-shelf magnification programs. Good places to start are the National Federation of the Blind (*www.nfb.org*) or the American Foundation for the Blind (*www.afb.org*). Screen magnification for the Mac, called inLARGE, is made by Alva Access Group, Inc., of Emeryville, CA (e-mail: *info@aagi.com*).

Chapter 9

Summary

As we near the end of our journey, let us pause and reflect upon how we as teachers can deliver education in a universally designed way. The guiding principle, as we saw in the Introduction and Executive Summary, is that it is up to educators and schools to take steps to reach out to nontraditional students. This means that educators need to plan for inclusion of such students. By taking a few fairly simple steps in advance, educators can broaden the appeal of offerings while containing costs; it is much more expensive to alter courses, texts, and other materials after-the-fact than before-the-fact. Chapter 3 identified three dimensions along which that effort may be made (Biermann, 1997):

- Learnability – how people acquire information (ease of learning, ease of use)
- Modality and medium – how people read (output) and write (input), and
- Nomadicity – networking or connectedness at a distance.

Briefly, universal design tells us to give students options. They should be able to obtain information in several ways, rather than just in one. This begins with information about the course itself. As suggested in Chapter 1, one reason higher education and adult and continuing education have not been as successful with minority-group members as with majority-group members is that the communication vehicles used to disseminate information about courses have not permeated minority communities as well as they have majority communities. In Chapter 5, another example was offered: you can tell your students where an electronic text version of the course textbook is available online. You can offer them disks containing your lectures. In both cases, these steps allow students to use speech synthesis (computer talking) to listen to rather than, or in addition to, reading. We want to present information in multiple ways—and to allow students to give us information in a variety of ways, as well. That is the key to "modality and medium," above. Speech recognition (Chapter 4) has matured to the point that it is a viable option for students who cannot type, or have difficulty writing in other ways. Finally, reaching students who are "nontraditional" simply because they live far away from a campus is now possible using distance learning (Chapter 6); reaching those who are nontraditional because of their peripatetic lifestyles, child-care responsibilities, or work schedules is also facilitated by the use of Web sites and the Internet in general (Chapter 8). The growing popularity of PowerPoint™ presentations illustrates an important point: teachers must take care not to say things that are not on the slides until after students have had a chance to read those slides. Even better is to read every word on every side out loud first, so that people with dyslexia or a vision impairment can "read" along with their classmates. Teachers should also slow down the pace of oral lectures, offer examples, and pause briefly before starting new topics. We should allow students to learn by doing, to work together on projects, and create multimedia or other presentations in lieu of taking a test, given that those activities serve learning. These measures help us to broaden appeal by embracing divergences in learning style.

Educators should take full advantage of emerging technologies so as to make learning even more universal than we can today. As this is written, long-distance and regional phone companies are installing massive amounts of fiber optic cable throughout the United States. Fiber can carry voice, data, and video—traditional voice calls, Web surfing and email, and full-motion video—all on one phone line, at one time. With the assistance of Bell Atlantic (now Verizon) and Adtran, a New York City communications firm, I demonstrated this integration at a conference at Hofstra four years ago (Bowe, 1996). Doing it then took weeks of hard work by highly trained technicians. Today, we are not quite at the point of simple "plug-and-play" but we are getting there. Why does this matter? I have a student in one of my classes now who had to be in Dallas when our class met two weeks ago. She missed the session and had to borrow notes. A year or two from now, she would be able to dial a phone number from her Dallas hotel room, and within minutes see me and her classmates as we sat in the Hofstra classroom; we could see and hear her, too. Another student was confined to bed by a serious illness, missing two weeks of classes. The same technology would have helped her to keep pace with her classmates.

Thanks to the 1996 Telecommunications Act (*www.fcc.gov*), public schools in every State in the nation now have internal wiring installed that connects desktop PCs to the World Wide Web—and facilitating two-way transmission of voice, video, and data. The pace of the change is nothing short of amazing. In 1995, in one of my textbooks, I wrote that, as of 1993, just 4% of American classrooms even had a phone jack and just 10% had enough electrical outlets into which to plug anything new (Bowe, 1995). Today, it is becoming a relative rarity to walk into a public school classroom and not see networked computers. Even elementary students are now producing multimedia projects that a few years ago would have challenged even professionals equipped with top-of-the-line dedicated production machines.

What will the next several years bring? The fact that fiberoptics can carry data as well as voice and video means that it can transmit *captions* along with full-motion video. This would open my course to far-away students who are deaf. It would have another benefit: students could actually walk over to a computer printer in the classroom and tear off a complete transcript of the day's lecture on their way out of the room. Using today's technologies, that transcript would offer my words, but not those of students asking questions or making comments: speech recognition that is truly "speaker independent" is not yet available on a continuous, or real-time, basis yet. When it comes, it will do more than give students a comprehensive transcript. It will actually change the way I teach in my own classroom: I could dial into the network and display the video feed on a monitor in the room, reading on that monitor captioned versions of what my students were saying, just a few feet from me. I now need a sign-language interpreter in the classroom to handle that translation. Someday, technology may do it for me. (It's not going to be next year, or even three years from now: the ability of computers to understand a multitude of different speakers, at real-time speed, is of the "someday" variety rather than the "here-and-now" variety.)

Appendix A

Instructional Media

In 1989, the Texas Legislature amended the state's textbook adoption statute to include electronic media. Two years later, the Legislature required publishers of textbooks that were adopted by the State Board of Education to provide not only the books themselves, but also computer files of those books so that these might be used to produce Braille versions of the texts. The Texas Education Code defines "electronic textbooks" as:

> computer software, interactive videodisc, magnetic media, CD-ROM, computer courseware, online services, an electronic medium, or other means of conveying information to the student or otherwise contributing to the learning process through electronic means. (Sec. 31.002[1])

Thus, Texas is one of two states (California is the other) to have had extensive experience in adapting instructional media for accessibility.

The following pages are excerpted from Chapter VI of the *Report on the Computer Network Study Project* (1999), a lengthy document produced by the Texas Education Agency's (TEA) Division of Textbook Administration. David Sharp, superintendent of the Lufkin Independent School District, chaired the project advisory committee. The full chapter was posted online by the Texas state rehabilitation agency for blind and visually impaired individuals at: *http://www.tsbvi.edu/textbooks/tea1999.htm*.

This document is revealing in the many features it discusses about electronic media. It then offers advantages of universal design with such media. Finally, it suggests strategies for making these media accessible to and usable by people with different learning styles, preferences, and disabilities. These strategies show how much the TEA has learned in the past decade about making instructional media accessible to people with different needs.

CHARACTERISTICS OF ELECTRONIC TEXTBOOKS (E–BOOKS)

At a minimum, electronic textbooks should be:

- **Perceivable**. The information that is presented in the book must be available in a form that can be perceived by the student. For example, if the student is blind then all of the information that is presented visually in the book should be available in another form such as audio that the student can use.

- **Operable and Navigable**. Students should be able to orient themselves and move within the electronic textbook. For example, a student has difficulty with eye-hand coordination (because of injury or disability). The student uses an electronic textbook, which requires a mouse or other pointing device to activate controls or navigation aids. Without an alternate means for navigating the control such as voice or keyboard control, the student would be unable to use the textbook.

- **Functional**. The textbook should provide the same function or benefit to the individual with a disability as it would to other students.

Electronic textbooks are made up of the same formatting and design elements as print textbooks, text formatting, symbolic text, graphics, and a navigation system. These formatting and design elements are enhanced because the information is presented electronically.

- **Text**. Text in electronic media may be resized, or the font may be changed to meet the reader's needs.

- **Text Formatting**. In addition to all the attributes of printed textbooks, text formatting in electronic textbooks may include hyperlinks which can move the reader to other parts of the page or book.

- **Symbolic Text**. Symbolic text in electronic textbooks may be resized or reformatted to meet the reader's needs. The student may be able to move symbols or edit equations to solve problems. The resulting solution could be dynamically graphed or displayed for additional student interaction.

- **Graphics**. The electronic versions of graphics may allow the image to be expanded to fill the entire screen, or sections of the image could be expanded to show detail. Graphs and charts may dynamically change to reflect student interaction or manipulation of associated data.

- **Navigation System**. Electronic textbooks use techniques for finding specific information within them, such as navigational maps, tables of contents with hyperlinks, heading levels, indices, and page numbers. They may also include hyperlinks, expand and collapse features, search functions, and interactive controls for navigating and controlling the information presentation.

Electronic textbooks may also include the following elements, which are not typical of print textbooks:

- **Hyperlink**. A hyperlink is a segment of text (word or phrase) or an inline image (an image displayed as part of a document) which refers to a location within the current document or another document (i.e., text, sound, image, or movie) elsewhere on the Web. When a hyperlink is activated or selected, the referenced document is retrieved from the Web and displayed appropriately. The electronic textbook may also include a "search" feature to find a specific word or phrase anywhere in the book. These navigation systems help the student find specific information (text, graphic, movie, or activity) in the electronic textbook.

- **Expand and Collapse Features**. Electronic textbooks also have the ability to expand or collapse their structure. For example, it is possible to produce a document which would collapse down to its major titles and subtitles. This makes it much easier to see the overall structure and to navigate to a particular level in the structure. Once that point is reached, it is possible to expand the structure exposing all of the paragraphs at that point. It is also possible to produce a document which provides a cursory treatment of all the material, but which allows the student to expand the information presented at any point in the document if he or she requires additional information.

- **Search Features**. Search features provide users with the ability to search documents and jump immediately to any occurrence of a particular word or phrase which is used. This capability also includes a "fuzzy" search capability, which allows an individual to search, for example, for the word "fish" and automatically find occurrences of the word "fish," "fishing," "mackerel," "trout," and "perch."

- **Sound**. Examples of this auditory information include prompts or warning sounds, music, spoken words, and natural sounds such as a lion's roar.

- **Fixed Sequence Animation and Movies**. Electronic textbooks may contain moving graphics. These may take the form of a simple diagrammatic animation or a full-color, high-resolution, graphic movie that may or may not be accompanied by sound.

- **Interactive Elements**. Electronic textbooks may contain visual graphic animation or symbolic interaction that can be controlled and manipulated by the student. [I]t is possible to show a four-stroke engine where the student can actually turn the flywheel controls forward and backwards at different speeds, study all of the workings of the engine, including the timing of the various events and mechanisms. More sophisticated simulations even allow students to carry out chemistry experiments where beakers, flasks, burners, and other apparatuses are manipulated on screen and the chemical reactions (e.g., color changes, heating, and explosions) occur on screen as they would if the real items had been manipulated. On a symbolic level, students could interactively change values in an equation describing lift properties of an airplane wing, and see how the wing changes shape and its effect on the flying ability of the airplane.

- **Live Information**. Electronic textbooks may contain hyperlinks to the Web that would provide students access to live information. For example, a science textbook could provide links to live weather information; a unit on volcanoes in a geography textbook could link to live seismographic information; or a biology textbook could link to "Chickscope," a live view of chicken embryo development within an egg.

- **Collaborative Environments**. Increasingly, education is becoming more collaborative. An electronic textbook could be designed giving students the ability to collaborate, through the use of "chat rooms," e-mail, discussion forums, or videoconferences. Students would be able to study with peers or a team to write reports, share research data, or share a "white board" or area on the screen where they can draw, write, calculate, or otherwise work together on the same "piece of paper." Through modern telecommunications, live people may be embedded in electronic textbooks. For example, touching an image in the electronic textbook would cause a communication link to be opened with a person—the teacher, other students, or perhaps a resource person somewhere else in the world studying a similar topic. The student would then be able to ask questions or interact with that individual. Essentially, a video teleconferencing session could be opened between the student and the teacher or resource person.

- **Three-dimensional or Immersive Environments**. An electronic textbook may include an immersive, three-dimensional environment or experience (commonly referred to as virtual reality). Depending on the rendering, these environments can be viewed, heard, felt and/or manipulated using various stereoscopic displays, three-dimensional sound systems, haptic interfaces and/or three-dimensional controllers. Ideally, these environments should simulate real world experiences without real world constraints. These simulated environments are used:

  - to replicate experiential learning, or practical demonstrations (e.g., a risk-free chemistry lab);
  - to allow the student to explore "what if" scenarios (e.g., what if we reduced the earth's gravitational pull);
  - to allow the student to experience otherwise impossible points of view (e.g., the backyard from the point of view of an ant);
  - to allow the examination and manipulation of simulated three-dimensional objects, which can be resized to suit the learning experience (e.g., viewing the heart from all sides or viewing a complex protein molecule);
  - to assist students in visualizing and understanding complex data that are not inherently visual or spatial (e.g., demographic effects of global warming on the Texas economy).

ADVANTAGES OF DIRECT OR BUILT-IN ACCESSIBILITY

The *Report* notes that the Telecommunications Act of 1996, PL 104–104, discusses "direct or built-in accessibility" vs. "compatibility with assistive technology devices." It then adopts those terms.

- **Cost**. Direct accessibility has advantages in cost, availability, and inclusiveness. When products are directly accessible to a student, schools do not need to deal with the added expense of acquiring special assistive devices to access and use the electronic textbook. Given the rapid changes in technologies, this also means that schools would not need to continuously buy new assistive technology devices as electronic textbooks evolved. Additionally, a directly accessible electronic textbook provides an enriched learning experience for all students.

- **Hardware Independence**. When accessibility is built in, students to not need to worry about whether their assistive technology will work with a particular computer...

- **Inclusiveness.** By using the same textbook and learning environments, all students will have increased interaction and collaboration with their peers. When students with a disability can directly use the same electronic textbooks and equipment, it is easier for them to work side by side with their peers who do not have disabilities.

- **Intuitiveness.** When access is built into electronic textbooks, it generally provides better and more intuitive learning experiences for the student with disabilities. Once the textbook has been opened, all of its functions should be usable without assistance.

ACCESSIBILITY REQUIREMENTS FOR ELECTRONIC TEXTS

- All electronic textbooks that are delivered via the Web must follow the content design principles established by the World Wide Web Consortium's Web Accessibility Initiative (WAI) Guidelines, including, but not limited to, WAI Page Author Guidelines, WAI User Agent Guidelines, and WAI Authoring Tool Guidelines.

- Use system tools whenever possible, including standard controls and standard text drawing routines. When this is not possible, use operating system tools (such as Microsoft Active Accessibility) to provide similar usability.

- All important information presented visually should also be available to the user in both auditory and text form. "Human voice" should be considered over synthesized speech whenever possible.

- All important information presented in audio must also be available in visual form. This should be provided as closed captions (with an indication of environmental sounds) and should include a text transcript. Movies could contain an optional sign language track.

- All important video or animated presentations should include audio descriptions of visual information for use by blind and visually impaired users. Including the text of the description for review would also be useful.

- Electronic textbooks should have the capability for increasing or reducing the speed of presentation, or pausing the presentation, to allow for different levels of comprehension.

- All controls should be operable in an efficient manner without a pointing device (e.g, a mouse). Providing keyboard commands for all important functions will support users who cannot use a mouse or who use alternative input devices, including speech recognition.

- All text should be user adjustable for font, size, and color.

- Users should be able to zoom in to view portions of the screen in more detail.

- Use established "standard" encoding such as Hyper Text Markup Language (HTML) and Extensible Markup Language (XML) for text; Graphics Interchange Format (GIF) and Joint Photographic Expert Group (JPEG) format for images; WAVE, QuickTime, Moving Picture Expert Group (MPEG), and Audio Visual Interleave (AVI) format for sound and video; and Synchronized Multimedia Interchange Language (SMIL) for sound, video, image, and text integration.

MAKING ELECTRONIC TEXTS ACCESSIBLE AND USABLE

Three methods are used to make text accessible in the visual interface. These are as follows:

*   **Synthesizing Speech from the User's End**. Electronic textbooks that use standard text drawing are compatible with standard screen reading software. Care must be taken, however, to ensure that the information is written to the screen in such a way that the individual can make sense of it using a screen reader. Screen readers typically scan horizontally across the screen.

*   **Building Audio into the Textbook**. When audio is provided with the textbook, there are fewer problems...However, if the audio presents information that is not available visually, it needs to be captioned or presented in some other visual form for students who are deaf or have hearing impairments.

*   **Screen Magnifiers**. Screen magnifiers are similar to screen readers in that they do not treat text in proprietary formats as text, but as "images." Therefore, when proprietary formats are used to create text, once magnified, the image may become grainy and unreadable. When standardized text drawing is used, the size of the text that is drawn to the screen is increased and the text is displayed in a larger font, maintaining its clarity.

Making symbolic information accessible involves use of Mathematics Mark–up Language (MathML), recently approved by the World Wide Web Consortium. The MathML code provides a standardized format for encoding mathematical equations that is independent of the final presentation media, be it print, audio, or Braille.

Search features [should include the capability to] search for character formatting or for structural items in the document. For example, the ability to search for the next title is very helpful for stepping through a document. If structure information is not available, the ability to search for the next bold or underlined text can be useful.

For students who are deaf or have hearing impairments, any information that is presented audiorially would need to be available in amplified form and as captions. For students who have both visual and hearing impairments, amplification may be helpful, but captions should also be provided in electronic form compatible with assistive technology so that they can be presented via Braille. The pace at which the auditory information is presented should be controllable to allow for different levels of comprehension. For example, it should be possible to speed up, slow down, stop, pause, or replay speech and captions. The techniques needed to provide captions for audio are the same as those described [below].

*   Electronic textbooks may contain full-motion video in color or in black and white, with or without sound. In order to make animation and movies accessible, the electronic textbook should provide:

*   Audio animations of the visual contents, which can be turned on and off as needed;

*   Captions of the auditory contents, which can be turned on and off as needed;

- The ability to back up and replay some or all of the information, to pause and restart from the same place, and to slow down the rate of presentation if, for example, a student needs more time to read the captions;

- An electronic version of the audio captions and the audio description text for use by students who are both visually impaired and hearing impaired.

These features can be provided in a number of ways. The same multimedia tools that are used to create the original presentation could be used to add additional audio description and captions to provide these features, and the ability to turn this information on and off could be built as part of the interface of the product. However, three popular multimedia players now provide the ability to handle audio description and captions within the media format. These formats are:

- QuickTime 3.0 and later.

- Microsoft SAMI (Synchronized Accessible Media Interchange) included in Microsoft Media Player version 5.2 or later.

- SMIL (Synchronized Media Integration Language), a format adopted by the World Wide Web Consortium. One SMIL player is the G2 player from RealNetworks.

For some electronic textbooks, it may be helpful to include supplemental materials such as tactile models, raised line drawings, Braille or audio materials which can provide orientation and information which would assist students who are blind or visually impaired to understand the graphic information or auditory descriptions.

Information that changes. Information may change for two reasons: (1) In response to an interaction with a student (e.g., the student adds a new substance to a chemistry experiment); (2) The information is "live" and is continually updated (e.g., a weather map is updated to show current conditions).

As mentioned earlier, two approaches can be used to make interactive programs accessible: direct accessibility or compatibility with assistive technologies. Technologies are now available that enable developers to design software which is compatible with assistive technologies, providing an important advance in the ability to create accessible software. These technologies are known as Applications Programming Interfaces (APIs). A possible compatibility solution for software built for the Windows platform is Microsoft's Active Accessibility (MSAA), an API for exposing elements of the screen and their state, including exposing the focus of the screen. Using MSAA, software developers can use entirely graphical custom interfaces while still making each element known to a screen reader. This makes it possible to provide access to every control and output of a simulation.

The growing popularity of Java as a programming language for the Internet has led to the development of the Java Accessibility API. With some similarities to MSAA, Java Accessibility allows software developers to expose the location, name, and state of each control while still using the graphical look-and-feel of their choice.

Virtual Reality and Three-dimensional or immersive environments. Wayfinding in a virtual world, with few constraints on travel, can be a daunting task even for a student with full vision. This situation may change dramatically with the development and broader availability of haptic interfaces and three-dimensional sound displays. "Haptics" is a term that encompasses both the sensing and action involved in touching and manipulating.

For many students, haptics is the preferred mode of exploration. Unlike the visual and auditory modality, by its very nature it is interactive. We manipulate the objects we are sensing in a continuous action–reaction loop. Thus, many people do not feel they have really "seen" an object unless they have handled it and explored it with their haptic sense. With the addition of haptic rendering and haptic display/control devices, three-dimensional, immersive environments will become more accessible and usable as additional display and control modalities become feasible and widely available. Wherever possible, electronic textbooks that include these tools should support multiple display and control modalities and provide information in redundant formats.

Appendix B

Resources

GENERAL RESOURCES

There are many resources on disability and education. Here are a few:

National Organization on Disability   (Source of Harris firm polling
910 16th Street NW   data reports)
Washington, DC 20006
www.nod.org

U.S. Bureau of the Census   (Source for U.S. Government data
Room 2312   on disability, age, ethnic groups, etc.)
Washington, DC 20233
1-301-763-8300
www.census.gov

U.S. Department of Education   (Source for U.S. Government data
Office of Special Education Programs   on special education)
400 Maryland Avenue SW
Washington, DC 20202
1-202-205-5465
www.ed.gov/offices/OSERS/OSEP

U.S. Department of Justice   (Source for information on the ADA)
 Office on Americans with
 Disabilities
P.O. Box 66118
Constitution Avenue NW
Washington, DC 20035
www.usdoj.gov

CAPTIONING

About a dozen for-profit and not-for-profit organizations offer captioning services. A useful site offering current contact information on captioners is: *http://www.erols.com/berke/alphalinks.html*. (It also has resources for doing your own captioning.) Here are six commercial captioners:

The Caption Center
WGBH-TV
125 Western Avenue
Boston, MA 02134
www.wgbh.org/caption

Captionmax, Inc.
530 N. 3rd Street
Minneapolis, MN 55401
www.captionmax.com

Caption Perfect
PO Box 12454
Research Triangle, NC 27709
www.members.aol.com/captioning/index.html

Henninger Digital Captioning
2601-A Wilson Blvd.
Arlington, VA 22201
www.henninger.com/hcap.html

National Captioning Institute
1900 Gallows Road #3000
Vienna, VA 22182
www.nicap.org

Vitac
4450 Lakeside Dr. #250
Burbank, CA 91505
www.vitac.com

E- BOOKS AND OTHER DIGITIZED MATERIALS

Recordings for the Blind   (Major source of e-books)
    and Dyslexic
www.rfbd.org

Project Gutenberg
www.promo.net.pg

(Offers e-text of children's
literature, adult literature,
and references)

BiblioBytes: Books on Computer
www.bb.com

(Has 350+ books for reading or
downloading)

Bookface.com
www.bookface.com

(Has books online for reading)

Children's Literature Web Guide
www.acs.uclgary.ca/~dkbrown/

(Lesson plans for teaching; classics)

Electronic Text Center
http://etext.virginia.edu

(Some 50,000 texts in 12 languages)

Etext Archive
www.etext.org

(Fiction, politics, poetry, etc.)

Internet Public Library
www.ipl.org

(Links to science, history, etc. texts)

On-Line Books Page
www.cs.cmu.edu/Web/books.html

(Books to read online. Index of 8,000
books, plus directories, archives, etc.)

Bookdigital
www.bookdigital.com
other

(Has some books, magazines, etc.,
that are readable online, plus links
to sites)

ACCESS TO E-TEXTBOOKS

JavaSoft   (Java Access API)
www.javasoft.com/products/jfc/accessibility/doc/what.html

Microsoft   (SAMI)
www.microsoft.com/enable/products/multimedia.htm

JustSMIL   (SMIL guidelines)
www.justsmil.com

W3 on SMIL   (W3's SMIL guidelines)
www.w3.org/TR/WD-smil

FREE AND LOW-COST PCs

National Cristina Foundation
www.cristina.org
e-mail: *ncf@cristina.org*

(Not-for-profit foundation that gets PCs from companies and people, distributes them to low-income individuals who have special needs)

PHYSICAL ACCESSIBILITY

U.S. Architectural and
 Transportation Barriers
 Compliance Board
1331 F. Street NW Suite 1000
Washington, DC 20004-1111
www.access-board.gov

(Source on federal design specifications.)

American National Standards
 Institute
11 West 42nd Street
New York, NY 10036
www.ansi.org

(Source on voluntary design specifications, including the 1998 ANSI A117.1 Standard for Accessible and Usable Buildings and Facilities)

Center for Universal Design
North Carolina State University
Box 8613
Raleigh, NC 27695-8613
www.design.ncsu.edu/cud

(Source on housing, etc., and on universal design in general)

Trace Research & Development
 Center
University of Wisconsin-Madison
590 Research Park Blvd.
Madison, WI 53719
www.trace.wisc.edu/

(Source on technology and disability and on universal design)

TEACHING RESOURCES

Blackboard
www.blackboard.com

(A free service letting teachers add online resources to their courses or host a course online. Knowledge of HTML is not required, a big plus.)

Distance Learning Clearinghouse
www.uwex.edu/disted/home.html

(Information on technologies, laws, courses and programs)

ERIC
http://ericir.syr.edu/ERIC

(A free source for AskEric, the public document-retrieval source)

International Society for Technology
in Education
www.iste.org

(Help for K-12 teachers and administrators.)

Pedagonet
www.pedagonet.com

(Has sites organized by subject so teachers may share resources, approaches)

Pepsite
www.microweb.com/pepsite

(Reviews of software and products for children, parents and educators)

Proteacher
www.proteacher.com

(Online curricula resources)

Resources for Educational
Technologists
http://magic.usi.edu/educ568/list.html

(Associations, news journals, Web sites, etc., listed with links)

Special Education Resources on
the Internet
www.hood.edu/seri/serihome.html

(Information related to special education)

Lernout & Hauspie
www.lhsl.com

(Language translation, speech recognition, and speech synthesis)

UNIVERSAL DESIGN

Adaptive Environments Center
"Images" Collection
www.adaptenv.org/udpictpg/udictrs.htm

(Pictures of good architectural and physical designs)

IDEA Center, SUNY-Buffalo
"Gallery of Bright IDEAs"
www.ap.buffalo.edu/~idea/BrightIDEA

(Architecture and design of consumer products)

J. L. Mueller, Inc.   (Consultant on universal design)
4717 Walney Knoll Court
Chantilly, VA 20151
jlminc@monumental.com

Leonard R. Kasday, Ph.D.   (Consultant on universal design)
Universal Design Engineer
Institute on Disabilities/UAP
Temple University
Ritter Hall Annex, Room 423
Philadelphia, PA 19122
kasday@acm.org

National Center on Dissemination of (Resource on research reports)
  Disability Research
"Doorways to Disability Research,"
universal design section
www.ncddr.org/doorways/univd

The Lighthouse   (Features a strong National Center for
www.lighthouse.org   Vision and Aging)
email: *aging&vision@lighthouse.org*

Trace R&D Center   (Very broad, helpful site)
University of Wisconsin at Madison
"Portfolio of Universal Design Examples"
www.trace.wisc.edu/world/

References

Almanac of Higher Education, 1998-99. American Council on Education. *http://chronicle.com/free/almanac/1998/almanac.htm.*

Aronson, D. and E. Colet. (1997). "Reading problems: From lab to cyberspace?" *Behavior Research Methods, Instruments, and Computers,* 29(2): 250–255.

Assembly Bill AB 422, "Instructional Materials; Disabled Students." Chapter 379. (Adds Section 67302 to the Education Code, State of California.) Signed by Governor Gray Davis, September 15, 1999.

Americans with Disabilities Act. Public Law 100–336. Enacted July 26, 1990.

Assistive Technology Act. Public Law 105–394. Enacted November 13, 1998.

Bailey, R. (1999). 3-day 1999 Annual User Interface Seminar. *www.humanfactors.com/annua.htm.*

Bar, L. and J. Galluzzo. (1999). *The Accessible School: Universal Design for Educational Settings.* Berkeley, CA: MIG Communications.

Biermann, A. W. (Ed.)(1997). *More Than Screen Deep: Toward Every-Citizen Interfaces to the Nation's Information Infrastructure.* Washington, DC: National Academy Press. *http://books.nap.edu/catalog/5780.html.*

Bowe, F. (1996). *Access to the Information Superhighway.* Report of a Conference. Hempstead, New York: Hofstra University.

Bowe, F. (1995). *Birth to Five: Early Childhood Special Education.* Albany, New York: Delmar.

Bowe, F. (1978). *Handicapping America: Barriers to Disabled People.* New York: Harper & Row.

Bowe, F. (1984). *Personal Computers and Special Needs.* Berkeley, CA: Sybex Computer Books.

Bowe, F. (2000). *Physical, Sensory, and Health Disabilities: An Introduction.* Columbus, OH: Prentice Hall/Merrill Education.

Bradsher, K. (1999). "As U.S. Buyers Age, the Auto Industry Makes Subtle Changes." *New York Times,* March 1, online edition.

Bremner, F. (1998). "On-line college classes get high marks among students. Cyber courses handy but more work for teacher." *USA Today,* November 16: p. 16E.

Brown, S. (1999). "How great machines are born." *Fortune,* March 1: 164[C] –164[D], 164[F]–164[G].

Carvajal, D. (1999). "Racing to Convert Books to Bytes." *New York Times,* December 9, online version.

Corballis, M. (1997). "The genetics and evolution of handedness." *Psychological Review,* 104(4): 714–727.

DiPierro, C., G. Nachman, and B. Raderman. (2000). "Screen size and Web browsing." Available online: *www.otal.umd.edu/SHORE/bs03*

Dirr, P. (1999). "Distance and Virtual Learning in the United States." In Farrell, G. (Ed.). *The Development of Virtual Learning: A Global Perspective.* London: The Commonwealth of Learning, p. 48.

Distance Education: Access Guidelines for Students with Disabilities. Sacramento, CA: Chancellor's Office, California Community Colleges. *www.htctu.fhda.edu/dlguidelines.*

Duarte, E., & Smith. S. (2000). *Foundational Perspectives in Multicultural Education.* New York: Addison Wesley Longman.

Ford, R. (2000). "Auto Designs for the Ages: Marketers Appeal to Boomers, Young Drivers." *Boston Globe,* March 5, A01.

Friedman, S. (1999). "Age isn't a barrier to computing, but bias is." *Newsday,* October 23: B6.

"Great Designs." (1999). *Fortune,* 164, March 1: 164.

Gutierrez-Clellan, F. (1999). "Mediating literacy skills in Spanish-speaking children with special needs." *Clinical Forum,* 30: 285–292.

Harry, B., M. Kalyanpur, and M. Day. (1999). *Building Cultural Reciprocity with Families: Case Studies in Special Education.* Baltimore, MD: Brookes Publishing.

Individuals with Disabilities Education Act. PL 102–15. Enacted June 12, 1997, amending PL 94–142, the Education for All Handicapped Children Act of 1975.

Intons-Peterson, M., P. Rocchi, T. West, K. McLellan, and A. Hackney. (1999). "Age, testing at preferred or nonpreferred times (testing optimality), and false memory." *Journal of Experimental Psychology: Learning, Memory and Cognition,* 25(1), pp. 23–40.

Johnson, K., & Morris, S. (1999). "Voice recognition: Will it work for you?" *www.wata.org/pubs/Articles/voicerec.htm*

King, T. (1999). *Assistive Technology: Essential Human Factors.* Needham Heights, MA: Allyn & Bacon.

Kleiber, P. B., M. E. Holt, and J. D. Swenson. (1998). The Electronic Forum Handbook: Study Circles in Cyberspace. *www.cpn.org/sections/tools/manuals/electronic_handbook1.htm*

Lewis, J. (1999). "Effect of error correction strategy on speech dictation throughput." *Proceedings of the Human Factors and Ergonomics Society,* 457-461.

Lubman, D. (1999). "Classroom acoustics." *Universal Design*, 4(4), October, 1, 8.

Mace, R., G. Hardie, and J. Place. (1991). "Accessible Environments: Toward Universal Design." In W. E. Preiser, J. C. Vischer, and E. T. White (Eds.). *Design Intervention: Toward a More Humane Architecture*. New York: Van Nostrand Reinhold.

Mace, R., *et al.* (1997). "The principles of universal design." Version 2.0. 4/1/97. One-page publication available from Center for Universal Design, School of Design, North Carolina State University, Box 8613, Raleigh, NC 27695-8613.

Margolin, M. (1999). "The Web isn't for everyone—yet." *www.hotwired.com/webmonkey/html/tutorials/tutorial1.html*.

McNeil, J. (1993). *Americans with Disabilities: 1991–1992. Data from the Survey of Income and Program Participation*. Current Population Reports, P70–33. Washington, DC: Department of Commerce, Bureau of the Census.

McNeil, J. (1997). *Americans with Disabilities: 1994-1995*. Current Population Reports, P70–61. Washington, DC: Department of Commerce, Bureau of the Census.

Mead, S., R. Spaulding, B. Sit, R. Meyer, and N. Walker. (1997). "Effects of age and training on World Wide Web navigation strategies." *Proceedings of the Human Factors and Ergonomics Society 41st Annual Meeting*. 152–156. [Human Factors and Engineering Society, P.O. Box 1369, Palo Alto, CA 90406. *www.hfes.org*.]

Microsoft Issues Guidelines for Making User-friendly Web Sites for All Ages. *www.microsoft.com/seniors/content/pr99/webdesign_pr.asp*

Miller, S. (1996). "Universal Design–And Beyond: Toward Multifunctional Use by Everyone." Paper presented at the Leadership Forum on Excellence in New York State Education, Albany, NY, February 1–2. Copyright Steven E. Miller.

National Disability Law Reporter, 10(6). Exchange of letters from Senator Tom Harkin to Deval Patrick, U.S. Department of Justice, and Patrick's reply to Harkin.

"New Girl in Town" (1999). July 16, *www.atmmagazine.com*.

Obiakor, F. (1999). "Teacher expectations of minority exceptional learners: Impact on 'accuracy' of self-concepts." *Exceptional Children*, 66(1): 59–63.

Open eBook Authoring Group. (1999). Open eBook Publication Structure 1.0. Final version. *www.openebook.org/*

Parette, P. (1999). "Transition and assistive technology planning with families across cultures." *Career Development for Exceptional Individuals*, 22(2): 213–231.

Pirkl, J. (1994). *Transgenerational Design, Products for an Aging Population*. New York: Van Nostrand Reinhold/International Thomson Publishing.

Reagan, J., & Trachtman, L. (Eds.). (1998). *Designing for the 21st Century: Proceedings*. Conference at Hofstra University, June 17–21, 1998. Raleigh, NC: Center for Universal Design, North Carolina State University.

Rehabilitation Act. Public Law 93–112. Enacted September 26, 1973.

Reib, M., and G. Reib. (1998). "Ear preference: Association with other functional asymmetries of the ears." *Perceptual and Motor Skills*, 86: 399–402.

Salend, S., and L. Taylor. (1993). "Working with families: A cross-cultural perspective." *Remedial and Special Education*, 14, 25–39.

Sciarra, D. (1999). *Multiculturalism in Counseling*. Itasca. IL: F. E. Peacock.

Sciarra, D., & Ponterotto, J. (1991). "Counseling the Hispanic bilingual family: Challenges to the therapeutic process." *Psychotherapy*, 28(3): 473–479.

Shedroff, N. (1997). "Interfaces for understanding." In Biermann, A. (Ed.) (1997). *More Than Screen Deep: Toward Every-Citizen Interfaces to the Nation's Information Infrastructure*. Washington, DC: National Academy Press.

Simmons, T., and M. Manahan. (1999). "The effects of monitor size on user performance and preference." *Proceedings of the Human Factors and Ergonomics Society*, 43: 1393.

Steinfeld, E. (1994). "The Concept of Universal Design." Speech presented to the Sixth Ibero-American Conference on Accessibility, June 19, Rio De Janerio. *www.ap.buffalo.edu/~idea/publications*

Story, M. F., and J. L. Mueller. (1998). "Measuring usability: The principles of universal design." In J. Reagan and L. Trachtman (Eds.). *Designing for the 21ˢᵗ Century: Proceedings*. Raleigh, NC: Center for Universal Design, North Carolina State University, 126–129.

Suhm, B., B. Myers, and A. Waibel. (1999). "Model-based and empirical evaluation of multimodal interactive error correction." *CHI 99 Conference Proceedings*, 584-591.

Telecommunications Act of 1996. Public Law 104-104. Enacted February 8, 1996.

Tindall-Ford, S., P. Chandler, and J. Sweller, J. (1997). "When two sensory modes are better than one." *Journal of Experimental Psychology*, 3(4): 257–287.

U.S. Architectural and Transportation Barriers Compliance Board. (1999). Americans with Disabilities Act Accessibility Guidelines for Buildings and Facilities; Notice of Proposed Rulemaking. *Federal Register*, November 16. *www.access-board.gov*

U.S. Department of Labor. (1999). *Futurework: Trends and Challenges for Work in the 21ˢᵗ Century*. Washington, DC: Author.

Universal Design. *Research Connections*, Fall 1999, 5. *http://www.cec.sped.org/osep/recon5/rc5cov.htm*

Vanderheiden, G. (1997). "Nomadicity, disability access, and the every-citizen interface." In Biermann, *op cit.*

Vanderheiden, G. (n.d.). "Principles of Universal Design." *www.trace.wisc.edu/world*

Vanderheiden, G. (n.d.) "Thirty-something (Million): Should They Be Exceptions?" *www.trace.wisc.edu/docs/30-some.*

Williams, J. M. (1999). "From NASA, a Web search tool for the blind." *Business Week Online*, Assistive Technology Column, September 29 *www.businessweek.com*

Williams, J. R. (1998). "Guidelines for the use of multimedia in instruction." *Proceedings of the Human Factors and Ergonomics Society 42nd Annual Meeting.* 1447–1451.

Index

About the Author

FRANK G. BOWE is Professor and, from 1995 to 2000, was Special Education Coordinator at Hofstra University. Professor Bowe is widely regarded as the "father" of section 504 of the Rehabilitation Act of 1973, which required accessibility in K–12 and college education. Among his earlier books are *Physical, Sensory, and Health Disabilities* and *Birth to Five: Early Childhood Special Education.*

DATE DUE